The Science of Everything

Everything for a Reason Series Book 4

By: Julie Edgington

Dedicated to:

For Manie

You are my hero

Love Mom

TABLE OF CONTENTS

CHAPTER 1

WHAT I THOUGHT I KNEW

"Your life can change in an instant. That instant can last forever."
[Laura Kasischke]

As I sat slumped in pain on the steps, I stared hypnotically at the old, brown 80's style carpet and everything around me was silent for a moment. I held my extremely large, pregnant belly, thinking I was going to die from the pain. Everything around me seemed to move in slow motion, though I was distinctly aware of one event unfolding in real-time: I could hear my eleven year old daughter's bedroom door slam shut.

Russell, my boyfriend, helped me up from the stairs.

"How could she do this?" he asked, in disbelief.

"I don't know," I said. "I was wondering the same thing myself."

Haley, my own child, my sweet little girl who had been through thick and thin with me, kicked me in my stomach in a preteen fit of rage. She seemed to be mad all the time now.

My own mother had passed away when I was Haley's age and so I had spent my preteen years without mother. As an adult, I simply had no frame of reference for how to navigate a mother-daughter relationship during these tumultuous years. I spent most of my life just surviving and not planning for the future. I had no idea about taking time to establish a long lasting relationship with anyone. Up until this point, my relationships with my three children consisted of us surviving and me taking care of their every need. I didn't have to deal with complicated preteen emotions; at least I hadn't had to yet, until now.

I thought of my children as well-behaved, especially Haley, until she began to turn, that is. I say "turn" because there is really no other way to describe what happens when you see your sweet little girl "turn" into a raging, emotional teenager. Watching her "turn" brought to mind images from paranormal TV shows I had seen, complete with werewolves and perhaps the Devil himself. Turning looks like evil incarnate, and it's so hard to believe your eyes when you are seeing such horror in the words and actions of your own child.

The day she kicked me in my stomach was a nightmare, not just for me but for our family. That day marked a dividing line, after which things between us were not the same. I ended up being perfectly okay once I could catch my breath again and the pain subsided, but I think this nightmare took Haley past a point she could never come back from. From that point on, she started to see herself as an abusive person, like her father. I still loved her the same, but I know she loved herself a little differently after that day, no matter how much I told her I forgave her for kicking me.

What we were going through was normal. At the time though, I couldn't see it that way. I felt such desperation and grief at what was erupting in my previously beautiful relationship with my daughter, as if I was the first mother in the world to go through such angst. What's more, though Russell and Haley hadn't had a great relationship up to this point, their relationship was even more strained afterwards.

Russell isn't her dad, she was never his sweet little girl, and now she had tried to hurt his child. He would never forgive her it seemed, yet he still took care of her when her own father wouldn't. Despite his care for her, Haley persisted in hating Russell for reasons that must only make sense to a preteen with a step-parent. "You're not my dad!" was a common phrase she spat at him, knowing those words cut as sharp as razor blades.

In an attempt to be the victim, Haley has always claimed Russell pulled her down the stairs after she kicked me in the stomach. He did grab her leg because he thought she was going to do it again, but let her go when he realized she was trying to run to her room.

Despite what was happening with Haley and despite having only recently heard my brother was being sentenced to 10 and a half years in prison for dealing drugs, I was happy. Believe me, as most people who could see my life then would agree, there was very little to be happy about; but I had accepted that life was just going to be miserable, and found some measure of happiness in that acceptance. I had always felt there was more to life than what I had been living, but at 27 years of age I had accepted the cards I was dealt: Mom dying when I was a little girl; finding out my dad was alive when I was 21, only to be rejected again by him, a preacher no less; my sister's and my brother's selfish acts which had harmed me immensely for years; abuse from boyfriends in the past; heck, I was even coming to terms with the sexual abuse I had to suffer through as a child.

For those who have read this book series sequentially, yes, up until this point I haven't addressed in any of my books that I was abused. It isn't something that I even want to admit to myself really, but it happened. At the time it was just one more thing to add to the long list of what I had gone through in life. I was always going to be "poor little Julie," in my own mind. It was just who I was and nothing could change it. I was always going to be the abused victim; abandoned, depressed, stuck, insignificant, weird, stupid, poor little Julie.

I wasn't worried about any of that though. I wasn't worried about it because I always knew all of it was going to be there. I could use it as an excuse if I had to. I could always blame my shortcomings on my past, so it was like a safety net. Safety nets are good, right?

One thing I did worry about was my baby. I knew he was going to be a boy and I knew he was healthy from the ultrasound, but I still worried. One thing and one thing only in this world which has always made me feel pure happiness is my babies and making sure they are okay.

This was my fourth child. I should have been a pro at being pregnant by now. I still worried. I went to my doctor, Dr. Pranger, who was quite the opposite of me in that he has a pervasive "suck it up, buttercup" kind of attitude. He had delivered my third child, Griffith, so I had known him for a while by that point. Although at one point during my pregnancy with Grif, I had hated the idea of going to him because we were so different. But something made me stay and now I was glad I did. We had become friends. He is just a couple years older than me and although he is a doctor, there were times I think he looked for validation from me that he was normal. He and his wife would go through some of the same things I was going through with my kids and we would talk about our observations and experiences with things like potty training and life in general. He often teased me about trying to keep up with him and his wife since they had five kids and I was creeping up on them with my fourth. Once we got to know each other a little better, we had a nice balance in our friendship. I would go in and complain about something, he would tell me I was fine and tease me a little before sending me home. He did give me a couple of ultrasounds to ease my mind and everything looked fine. I was just a worry wart, he said.

The feeling of something being wrong in my pregnancy overwhelmed me at times to the point I would began to plan what I was going to do when I discovered something had happened to my baby. I should probably point out that I had thoughts like this while pregnant with my other children, so it wasn't completely abnormal for me. Mostly I found that if I kept busy, I wouldn't think of such things. There were plenty of reasons to stay busy – I had a one year old to take care of and my eight year old daughter, Alex; also there was Haley and her preteen drama. It all kept me busy enough.

Then eventually Russell did the unthinkable. He made the mistake of trying to be intimate with someone else and I found out about it. He didn't do anything with her, but I put it in my mind that things were over and knew I would probably leave after I had the baby. I had been secure and had gotten too happy in life. My limited beliefs surrounded me like an echo. The sadness of what I had gone through ate away at my soul, though I tried hard to enjoy life. I knew I had one thing I could do in this world and I was good at it. I was a mom and that made me belong in this world.

Not for one second did I think I was doing everything right as a mother, but I knew I loved my children. I was never going to let anything hurt my kids the way I had been hurt. Physically and emotionally, I was their protector. This purpose was what I focused on and it is what kept me going in life. As long as I could be in control of every aspect of what was going on around us, then I could prevent life from taking them like it had taken me. They couldn't be victims like I was; I wasn't going to allow it.

I laugh at the thought about how we trick ourselves into thinking we are so in control of everything. There is one thing that has control in this world and it is the certainty that the things that are supposed to happen, will. You could sit on your couch all day long, forever, and those things that are prewritten will happen somehow and in some way. You can, of course, add to your experience here on earth, but you can never take the lessons out of it. You can't take away your purpose here.

My life was about to change forever. Everything I had known about life and depression was gone in an instant. This one gift God would bring me would make me stop feeling sorry for myself forever. I would never look at life the same way again. I would find my reason for living and know I have purpose here on this earth.

My gift came two days before my due date. I had been having contractions, but nothing regular. Russell came home for lunch and I told him I thought it was time, but I was going to wait a little while and I would call him at work if I needed him. Russell left to go back to work and I knew he would be coming home sooner than later. I was right, and next thing I knew Russell was rushing home to take me to the hospital.

I was so relieved that finally I would meet and hold this little baby in my arms.

Dr. Pranger showed up at the hospital shortly after Russell and I arrived. I could hear his distinctive, chipper voice as he walked down the hall towards my room. Then, before I knew it, there stood my tall, slender, well-groomed doctor. He stood there, looking at me in the doorway of my room, and knowing he was there brought a welcome relief. We joked around and talked for a little while. We were both comfortable with each other by that point, as we had already done this once before when Grif was born. I felt a little weird about having a baby with a different guy, and only a year and 10 months after my third child was born. Even though Dr. Pranger is a devout Catholic, he never made me feel like I should be ashamed of my life in any way.

"If you could have this baby by 7:30 that would be great, I have a volley ball game tonight," Dr. Pranger said with a huge smile on his face.

Laughing and in a cocky tone, I replied, "I will get right on that!"

Moments later, the good doctor broke my water. I noticed a look on his face then. It was the look of someone who knows something is wrong, but they are intent on pretending everything is alright. It was a look I had never seen before on Dr. Pranger's face. The corners of his mouth pointed down, almost making him look like a completely different man.

"What is it? Is there something wrong?" I knew the answer before he even said anything.

"There is meconium in the water," he said. He went on to explain that my baby had a bowel movement while still inside the womb, which can be a sign of possible complications such as the meconium getting in the baby's airway and causing infection.

Dr. Pranger perked up a little then and did not seem quite as worried, and I relaxed slightly. As I said before, he never worried unnecessarily about anything.

I was a little concerned, but I did not feel as if it was going to be a problem. Dr. Pranger walked out of the room, a spring in his step like his usual upbeat self, and a nurse came in shortly after. She inserted a hose next to the baby to help flush away the meconium and also affixed a monitor to the baby's head to his heart rate more efficiently. It was very uncomfortable and I had never had any of my children monitored like that before, so I was somewhat nervous.

Dr. Pranger came in a short while later to check on me and removed the monitor. He didn't seem too happy that the nurse had used that specific monitor. I was grateful for that because it was pinching me the whole time and I thought it was a horrible instrument to use on a baby, especially because it was actually screwed into his head!

Everything else was normal about my labor and delivery. The room was so calm and quite that night. I felt at ease for some reason, even though I was having a baby. I just couldn't wait to meet my little guy. Just like any other parent, I was excited. I kept looking at the clock thinking to myself how funny it would be if I actually had my baby by 7:30 so Dr. Pranger could make it to his game. That would show him how good I was at having a baby! It would be a good story to tell later on, I thought. How many woman can have a baby on a schedule?

After one and a half pushes and at 7:13 P.M. on March, 9th 2004, Manie was in the world! He was my biggest baby, weighing seven and a half pounds, and I think that is the reason I pushed him out in such a short time. It hurt so bad I just wanted him to be out! The doctor laid him on my belly and he started to cry. I was so relieved to finally see him. I smiled at the doctor and said, "I told you I would get you to your volleyball game."

Dr. Pranger just looked at me and smiled. It would be the last smile I would see from his face for a while.

One of the nurses was standing next to me and she began to wipe Manie off while he was still on my tummy. Manie's cries became louder and louder the harder she rubbed. It wasn't unusual to me at all, as I know babies are supposed to cry when they are born. Then I noticed the nurse was getting a little rough with my baby, almost as if she was becoming frantic. I knew that something was wrong. I grabbed a towel that was lying next to Manie and I started to help her clean him off. The nurse grabbed Manie from me and laid him in a bassinet a few feet from my bed. She demanded Dr. Pranger come to check on him right away. I asked what was wrong with my baby and the nurse ignored me.

Little did I know that, on that day, I gave birth to one of the greatest teachers this world will ever see, my son. I also gave birth to all new thoughts and beliefs that would lead me to my destiny and purpose. All of a sudden everything I had gone through in my life meant nothing and everything, all at the same time. In one breath, my life changed. I breathed in, I was still life's victim. I breathed out, nothing was about me anymore. In between that breath in and that breath out, I had seen it all as if I had stepped into some other dimension.

All of a sudden I knew everything that there ever was and ever will be, from the beginning of time to the end. Like a movie, I saw it all. In that in-between time, when I was nothing, it all made sense. I knew what I was about go through and I knew why everything had happened to me. I know it seems impossible that within a millionth of a second, between a breath in and a breath out, all of that could have happened, but it did. I had just been given insight. When I released the air from my lungs, all that I had just learned and witnessed left me, and I was human again. All I knew was that I had just been given something. I remembered enough to keep me going and to keep me searching. It all may have left me, but I could not forget what was given; even if for such a short time, I knew. At this very moment was when my point of view changed. Everything I had gone through was all for a reason, it all had purpose! I didn't matter anymore, yet I was the reason everything was happening. I was like a blind person seeing for the first time. The purpose of all the torture, loss, pain, abandonment and love was to prepare me for was about to happen. It's not often that people get to know directly what their purpose is, but I do and now I get to share it with you.

Welcome to my experience which made me realize everything happens for a reason!

CHAPTER 2

ALL AROUND ME, FLAMES

Life has many ways of testing a person's will, either by having nothing happen at all or by having everything happen all at once."
[Paulo Coelho]

My brief moment of enlightenment was just that, brief. Pulled from my thoughts by the sound of Manie crying, I glanced over to see Dr. Pranger and the nurses huddled around him. Sometimes time travels slower than in other times, and this was one of those instances. It really had just been minutes since the cord had been cut and he was separated from the warm comforting world he once knew, but time was creeping forward and seconds seemed to last for long minutes. His cozy place inside me was a world he was safe in, a world that protected him from the vicious place he had been born into, and I felt sad for him.

Although the lights were dim in my room, I was still able to discern Manie didn't have the nice peachy-pink color of a healthy newborn; rather, he was turning blue. The only way I can describe what I observed is to say he looked as if he had taken a bath in a blue raspberry slushy. It all happened so fast and before I knew it Dr. Pranger was leaning over me, whispering, "He is going to the nursery." Russell left my side then to follow Manie. My good friend Mary was there waiting with me and within seconds, she was gone too. She wouldn't tolerate the lack of information we were being given, she went to find answers.

I trusted in God, though I was moving into a delusional state of mind at that point. I began to rationalize what was happening. I made myself think that there wasn't anything seriously wrong with my baby, not my baby. My baby was going to be perfect no matter what. My internal conversation was one where I had convinced myself that indeed I had worried just enough when I was pregnant so therefore there was no way there could be anything really wrong with Manie. You always worry that you didn't worry enough and then, when it is over, you tell yourself how stupid it is to worry. It is natural to worry, especially if you are a mother.

Dr. Pranger walked into my room with a somber look on his face. He said, "It isn't clear yet what is wrong with Manie. A specialist is coming to look at him right away."

I could not find the courage to say even one word. I couldn't look at him and I avoided all eye contact. I wanted to cry and knew if I felt any human contact by looking into my friend's eyes, I might just loose the battle and the tears would flow. It is hard for me to cry - it shows weakness on the outside we feel on the inside - and I couldn't afford to be weak right now. Maybe if I could avoid the outward display of worry, weakness would also dissipate on the inside and I would feel strong again. Dr. Pranger, sensing I didn't want to talk, left me there lying in a muddle of disorder. I had no idea what was happening to my little guy. I kept telling myself over and over in my head that he was alright, and I think I was in shock because I just felt numb. Time had no meaning at this point.

Again Dr. Pranger entered my room, moments later, but this time he wasn't alone. By his side stood an older, more serious looking doctor I had not seen before. Both of them were trying to explain to me what was going on. No one, even the specialist, was certain what was wrong with Manie. Oxygen was not getting into his blood for some reason. The specialist explained it was likely a problem in either his heart or his lungs and though it could have been a complication from the meconium, it was even more possible that it was something more serious.

"He might have to be transported by helicopter to the University of Iowa Hospital," one of the doctors said. I was in a daze at this point, too much to realize who was talking.

Having grown up most my life in Waterloo, Iowa I knew the seriousness of what the words 'University of Iowa Hospital' meant. You don't get airlifted to the University of Iowa, in Iowa City, unless there is something horribly wrong. As they started to leave the room I looked up at Dr. Pranger and in an attempt to make me feel better he said, "Don't worry yet. I'll tell you when you can start to worry."

That was it! It was the reassurance I longed for! Dr. Pranger didn't tell me to worry yet! Everything was going to be alright. I knew as long as he didn't tell me to worry, I was just over-reacting. Of course the doctors were just making sure he was fine because of the meconium, that was it! Manie is going to be fine, I thought, which eased my own mind. He had to be fine, bad stuff happens in life to me, not to my children. I protect them so bad things don't happen. I was becoming very good at talking myself into a false sense of security. I knew the doctors were just trying to prepare me for the worst, just in case. I had talked myself into believing that the worst rarely happens. Even with the horrible life I had already had, the worst case couldn't happen.

I must have been moving in and out of reality because I wasn't sure how I ended up on the phone. I was talking to my older sister, Cindy. I could hear myself trying to explain what was going on. She kept telling me Manie was fine. I didn't want her to tell me something I already knew. I was mad at her for not being there with me, but I didn't tell her that. I just pretended I had to go, then hung up the phone.

As soon as I hung up, Dr. Pranger walked through the door again. I could feel sorrow coming from him and I could hear my own heart beat as he slowly said the words, "It is time to start worrying and if it was me, I would be worried."

My doctor, a man who never thinks anything is that bad, was telling me I needed to worry. The last bit of hope I had been hanging on to was gone. I had a knot in my stomach so big I thought I might just die. Russell came into the room just in time to hear the doctor tell us, "We aren't sure, but there might be something wrong with Manie's heart and he needs to be airlifted right away to Iowa City. The helicopter is on its way and will be here in a little while to get Manie."

With a big a burst of energy I blurted out, "Russell has an irregular heartbeat! It is because of him!" I do not even know why I said that. It just came out of my mouth without my permission. I did not mean to blame Russell, but my mind was going a thousand miles a minute. I was trying to think of things that would explain what was wrong with Manie. I thought if I could help them understand what was wrong, they would tell me that it was alright and he could stay there with me. My mind works in such a way that to me everything has to have an answer. I had to figure all this out and make it better because that is what I do. I don't let anything hurt my children. I fix everything and I was bound and determined to fix this too.

"Russell's irregular heart beat does not have anything to do with what is wrong with Manie," the doctor said, as if he felt sorry for Russell because I blamed him. With a sincere change in his tone Dr. Pranger tilted his head to get a better look at my face and said, "I will come right away in the morning to sign the release papers so you can leave." I had a million questions for the doctor, but I did not want to open my big mouth again and say something stupid. I just nodded my head in agreement and the doctor left the room.

Russell said, "I am going back out there to check on Manie." Again I nodded my head in agreement, and Russell left too.

I was sitting there by myself, stunned, in a horrible nightmarish daze. I felt as if I was going to be sick. I wanted to grab my baby and leave the hospital because the doctors were wrong and my baby was fine. I just kept watching the door and waiting for someone to come in with my baby and say they were sorry they made a mistake. It wasn't a matter of wishing it to happen, I just decided I wouldn't accept any other outcome.

The door did pop open and my heart jumped, thinking my demands to God to make my baby healthy worked! It was one of the nurses, but she did not have my baby. She was a younger nurse, probably in her early 20s. I am sure this was the first time she ever had anything like this happen during her shift. As she came in I could tell she was going to cry. She started to do her job of cleaning and tending to the messy room. It only took a couple of minutes before her human side got in the way and she asked while holding back tears, "Can I give you a hug?" I thought it was a bizarre request, but I gave her a short hug. The realization that there was something really wrong, even more than what the doctor had expressed to me, hit me fast. Emotions went through me like a freak flash flood. I felt scared and trapped like I could not do anything to get me or my baby out of this horror story.

After our brief hug the nurse said, "I will help you get up into a wheel chair in a few minutes. Then you can go see Manie before they take him to the other hospital."

Those were not the words I had wanted to hear. The nurse left the room and again I was alone. I sat there for a few minutes, which seemed like forever, and I think I was still going in and out of shock. I wanted to turn back the hands of time and stop labor and just be at home with my baby safe inside of me. I kept repeating over and over, "God make him alright. Please God, make him better." The more I would rerun the words, the more I felt like a small child begging for something she just knew she wasn't going to get, as if my words fell on deaf ears. Yet I continued to beg.

Most of the time while I was left alone I felt like a crazy person. Around others I felt cold hearted. I felt like everyone was expecting me to be hysterical, but I couldn't. In my head I was frantic, irrational and just plain mad, but the emotion would not go any further than my mind. It brought me back to that night when we went to see Mom in the hospital when she passed away. That little 11 year old girl I was then just stood there not being able to move, staring at her lifeless body, waiting for it to show some kind of expression of life. Now I was just sitting there again, stuck in my own mind, just watching, just waiting for a miracle. It was as if I was separated from my body and I was just there to watch and observe.

The nurse returned with a wheel chair and another nurse to help. They started to help me get up out of my bed. I had an epidural while I was in labor and it had worn off, but with everything that had happened I didn't notice when. As I started to move I could feel the pain of what my body had just gone through. I felt shaky, especially in my legs. I knew things were real now as my feet hit the solid floor and I felt the physical support of the bed I had been laying in, leave my body. I was now independent of where I was and now was moving forward regardless of my opinion.

I was empathetic to the sincerity of what the nurses were feeling. They handled me so gingerly as they helped me out of bed and the few feet to the wheelchair. I felt like a delicate, precious antique they were trying to pamper so as not to cause anymore scratches, as if they knew one more blemish might cause me to crumple to a pile of dust on the floor. The new nurse pretended that everything was normal and fine as she asked me about how long my hair was. I had extremely long, bleach-blonde hair that was pulled back into a large bun. I often loved comments about my long beautiful hair, but this time I could only muster lip service to give to the conversation. Words were coming from my mouth on automatic, and inside I was wondering how this woman could even think I'd be interested in talking about such a vain thing as my hair at a time like this, when seeing my baby was all that was on my mind. I knew why though; she didn't want to feed into the worry and the tension that was already in the air.

My wheel chair sat stationary, pointed towards the door. I was ready to roll down the hall to the nursery to see Manie and fix this before it got too out of control. I could feel hesitation coming from the nurses and soon found out why. Before we left my room, they began to warn me. They didn't stumble with their words. The nurse that had just been so talkative about my hair spoke first. "We want you to be prepared for what you are about to see," she said. "When you see Manie, he will have a tube down his throat and a catheter and IVs put in."

The younger nurse who had given me the hug earlier added to the statement by saying, "There will be a lot of wires and he is not awake."

"Okay," I replied.

We began our way out of my room and down the hallway. One nurse pushed the wheel chair as the other walked next to me. I was nervous about what I was going to see, but I knew I could make it all better, that is what I do. I was going to figure it out and Manie was going to be fine.

CHAPTER 3

SEEING STILL ISN'T BELIEVING

"There will always be a reason why you meet people. Either you need them to change your life, or you're the one that will change theirs." [Angel Flonis Harefa]

Russell's mom was holding Grif when we arrived at the nursery. His dad, sister, and brother were there, and so was Mary. She had been keeping a watchful eye on Manie for me. They were all standing at the big huge window that looked into the nursery, watching as the doctors and nurses interacted with my baby. But as the nurses and I walked toward them, everyone turned away to look at me instead. I could feel everyone's eyes glaring at me as I was slowly wheeled past them into the nursery.

Manie was in a section of the nursery that was separate from all of the other babies. His little hospital bed sat in the middle of nowhere, looking painfully small in the large space of the room. The nursery was old and seemed to not have been remodeled since the late 60s; everything had that same ugly tan or brown color. The tone of the room seemed to match everyone's mood, especially mine. The nurse parked my wheel chair next to Manie and backed away. I sat just below eye level to Manie's bed. I had to stretch my neck and sit forward a little just to see him completely.

I examined every inch of Manie's tiny, plump little body. I wanted to make sure everything I had been told was true. I started at his head; those were his dad's eyes. His eyes were closed as if he was sleeping,

19

just like the nurse had warned me he would be. He had been sedated so he would not feel any pain and so the air tube could be put down his throat. The tube protruded from his mouth and was taped to his face. His lip was being pulled by the air tube and looked like it could be ripped off at any moment. I alerted one of the nurses and was ignored. Overhearing my concern, a different nurse came over and moved the air tube slightly to give Manie's little lip some relief.

My gaze then moved down to Manie's chest, which stuck out and was tense as if he was arching his back, but he wasn't. I watched as his chest and stomach moved from breathing; it was the only sign of life I could see. There were his perfect little legs and feet. One of his arms was wrapped up with a board to protect the IV the nurses had put in. Despite having the extra oxygen, his limbs and body were still purplish blue in color. I drew my eyes back so I could see all of Manie at once. There were tubes and wires coming from just about every hole in his body and even some new ones the nurses had made.

I began to rub his little hand with my finger, desperately trying to bridge the distance and desperation I felt. All I kept thinking to myself was, how can I make this better for Manie? How would he know I was even there to protect him?

"Can I hold him before he leaves?" I asked, just in case they might have let me.

"No!" one of the nurses replied sharply.

The room was a buzz of activity as the nurses worked to prepare Manie to leave. I looked up at the clock and, in disbelief, realized it had only been a little over a half an hour since Manie had been born. How was that even possible? I felt I had lived lifetimes in those thirty, fleeting moments. What was time anymore? It really meant nothing to me now. When you are having fun and are happy, time seems to move fast; but now, in this nightmare, time seemed to be dead, like the meaning of it was something to be mourned.

Russell had been standing next to Manie's bed even before I was wheeled into the room. We couldn't even really look at each other. I knew if I looked at him I would probably lose it. Whatever "it" was, "it" would escape me if I looked at Russell and I would go completely insane right there.

Realizing all of Russell's family and Mary were still looking through the window to the nursery, I felt like an animal at the zoo or, even worse, a freak at the circus. It was if they were watching to see what we would do next. I just wanted everyone to go away and stop looking in on us and taking pictures. I spoke to Russell without looking at him. "Please tell them to go for a little while so we can have some time to ourselves before he leaves."

Russell heard me but didn't move away from Manie's side. I knew neither of us wanted to miss a moment. I pretended that no one was around as I reached up and touched Manie's hand and the side of his body, just to let him know I was there. I glanced over and looked at Mary standing behind the glass. She looked just as she always had: confident and poised. Her long blonde hair was curled to perfection, never was there a hair out of place. Her makeup was always done no matter what. It did not matter where she was or who she was with, she always fit in.

Just for one second our eyes caught and I dumped all these horrible feelings, every one of them, on her. When I saw Mary looking back at me, I felt relief. At least one person in this world knew exactly what I was feeling. She was there with me inside my heart where it was lonesome and confusing. I now know this was a transfer of some sort of energy. Yes, I know it sounds like something from a sci-fi movie, but it was real.

I would come to find out what the word friend really meant. It was as if God sent me Mary because He knew I would need someone there for me. I flashed back to that moment, years before, when I found her ghostly white dog in my front yard and thought about the way he made himself at home and refused to leave me until I found Mary. I knew in that moment, at Manie's bedside, that ridiculous dog had a purpose and now that purpose was going to be filled. Mary was with me to see me through my most difficult moment so I could see Manie through his.

With the extra little strength Mary had given me I turned and looked at Russell. His face was blank; I could tell he was unsure of what to do. Since I am so much older than him he has always looked to me for answers when he finds himself lost. I knew this time if he asked, I would not know what to tell him. I would not have any answers for his questions. I was hoping he realized I would not have the answer. For once I was hoping he could help me. He never did ask me what to do. Instead, I watched as Russell transformed from being a young man into something different, something wiser. From that moment on it wasn't just Russell that was different, I was too. There was no turning back; forever our lives would be changed.

The opening of the elevator doors just across the hall from the nursery stirred me from my thoughts. Looking up, I saw the medical technicians from the helicopter moving in our direction and I knew they were there to take Manie away. We watched as he was moved to a smaller, more portable bassinet with a dome around it. The techs were dressed in black jump suits and carried a lot of equipment with them. One of the technicians, a woman, said to me, "He will be very safe and we will take good care of him." I gave her a half smile, but I could not look her in the eyes. As they rolled Manie into the elevator, I said to him, "I love you."

It was the first time he had ever heard those words and I hoped in my heart it wouldn't be his last. I did not want to let him go and I could not go with him. I had to let them take my baby or he would, without a doubt, die.

I sat there in my wheel chair, pointed towards the elevator. As the doors closed I began to feel so empty and dead inside. All the rushing around and sense of emergency was gone. The feeling of everyone being exhausted took its place. I just continued to sit, stunned, in my wheel chair until someone began to push me to a new room somewhere in the maternity ward. Russell, Mary and Grif went outside and watched as Manie flew away in the helicopter. I had rarely left any of my children in the care of anyone but myself. I had a horrible fear someone would hurt them because, in my eyes, no one cared about them as much as I could. No one would look out for them and make sure they weren't abused or treated unfairly. Now I had no choice. My newborn baby was flying away in a helicopter to be with strangers, people who had never met me and who couldn't possibly understand how much I love my baby.

I was getting settled in my hospital room when Russell and Mary came back up to see me. Grif had left with Russell's parents. Mary came close to my bed and said, "I will leave right away for Iowa City."

"No, don't. You have to go to work," I replied. I really wanted her to go be with Manie, especially since I doubted anyone else would go. Russell's family just kept telling him, "Manie is going to be fine," and, "It's not a big deal." I was just going through the motions of being polite when I told Mary to not to miss work. I knew she would not leave my baby all alone.

I looked at Russell and I could tell he was terrified to drive all the way to the other hospital by himself, not knowing where to go or what to do. Once he knew that Mary would be there to help him, a look of relief came over his face. I did not care if I was going to be left all alone. I just wanted someone there for my precious baby. Knowing that Mary and Russell would be there for him would have to be enough for now. I knew in the morning I could leave and be there myself.

Before she left, Mary promised, "I will be there all night with Manie. I will be back here early in the morning to pick you up and take you to Iowa City."

I asked her one time. "Are you sure you want to do this?"

"Yes. Don't worry about it," she confirmed, as though her act of kindness was nothing at all.

I often wonder how I got so lucky to have such a wonderful caring friend. To this day I thank God that we found each other and that my life is graced with her friendship. Once Mary and Russell began to walk out the door the words "everything happens for a reason" echoed through my mind.

Again I thought about Mary's dog and how he brought my friend back to me. Then I thought about what Mary and her family had gone through a few years before. Her nephew had been killed by his father. The family suffered so horribly.

I thought about the time they had spent in Iowa City at the hospital and I remembered going to the hospital with Mary and talking to her sister. As her sister's three month old baby had laid there, I had felt a need to make things better for her somehow and said, from a place of desperation, "Everything will be okay." I regretted that moment and I felt those words probably made her sister hate me. Why did I think I had the power to make things better for her? Now I knew it wasn't my place to make it all go away. I didn't want anyone to comfort me like that and she probably hadn't either.

As I lay in my bed I thought about what it felt like in the hospital that night when I was with the baby, Mary and her sister. I thought about how my son was the one laying in that bed now. I thought about how, back then, I was able to walk away from it and go home after leaving my words with the poor heartbroken mother. I just wanted to make things better for her as she watched her baby suffer. But now it was my turn.

As bad as it was to think this, I considered that Mary had gone through a similar pain with her own sister and nephew and without that, perhaps she would not have been able to understand my own pain. She wouldn't be the person I needed her to be. Manie and I might not have been the reason for their heartache, but you can put a purpose or a reason to something bad after it happens. They had to go through what they did for their own reasons, but we were recipients of a small piece of what that tragedy left behind – compassion and understanding. Finding a reason after something horrible has happened gives us hope and the ability to continue on with a little less pain.

CHAPTER 4

HOW DO I DO THIS?

"There is a sacredness in tears. They are not the mark of weakness, but of power. They speak more eloquently than ten thousand tongues. They are the messengers of overwhelming grief, of deep contrition, and of unspeakable love." [Washington Irving]

I was alone in my hospital bed. I don't just mean there was no one in my room, it was more than that. The aloneness I felt went beyond the physical realm; and it weighed me down with its enormity.

By alone I mean there wasn't a soul on earth or anywhere else who knew exactly what I was going through, not even my friend Mary. I was also alone in the sense that everyone had left the hospital. Dr. Pranger was gone, Mary, Russell, his family – they had all scattered in different directions.

For the first time since Manie's birth, I thought about crying and I was mentally preparing to let myself cry. The emptiness of being so alone, combined with the anxiety and grief surrounding Manie's birth, left me feeling sick in the deepest part of my soul. I knew I had to release those feelings somehow and crying seemed like a logical next step. It wasn't enough though, to cry. No, what I really wanted to do then was die. But I could not do that to Manie, who had already gone through so much in his short life.

The shock I had been through had put up an instant wall around my heart, keeping it contained so it wouldn't explode into a billion little pieces. I started to feel the shock escape me and I knew I could cry now. As I began to feel my eyes start to swell, but before that first tear had a chance to completely form, a nurse popped her head into my room and said, "You have an important call, pick up the phone when it rings. It is a doctor from Iowa City."

The sound of the nurse's voice sent my newly forming tears into retreat. A few seconds later, the phone rang. I reached for the phone but was overcome with nervousness; my heart beat in my chest so intensely I could feel it throughout my whole body, even down to the very tips of my fingers and toes.

If you have read my previous book Love of an Angel you know I have a phobia of talking on the phone. It rang again and I could feel my throat swell and my mouth became dry. I tried to swallow, but my throat was paralyzed and no matter how hard I tried, I struggled to be able to pick up the receiver. Instead I took a very deep breath. With a slow exhale, I wrapped my trembling fingers around the corded, beastly thing called a telephone. It was the same ugly tan color as everything else in the hospital. I picked up the receiver and placed the cold hard plastic to my ear. There was that familiar slow motion feeling again, the one that had been way too frequent in my life, the same exact feeling I had felt when I picked up the phone in the middle of the night knowing it was my brother–in–law calling to say my mother had died.

"Hello?" I answered with a crackle in my voice.

I heard the sound of a woman's voice on the other end. She explained very quickly she was a doctor from Iowa City. In the most serious and firm voice I have ever heard, she said, "Listen to me very carefully. I will explain to you what is going on quickly, and then I will need for you to give your consent over the phone. When I ask you if you give your consent, I will tape record your response. Do you understand?"

The urgency in her words now made time speed up faster than what

I knew was humanly possible. There was no time to think, and I felt as though I was barreling at top speed down a track that would lead to an unavoidable collision. What if time was moving so quickly I wouldn't be able to hear her correctly? What if I missed an important detail? What if I didn't understand or, even worse, what if I forgot what she said because she was speaking so fast? For all the angst I had felt when time had crept slowly by only moments before, there was nothing I would not have done to slow it down now. There was no time to analyze the situation or even think about all the options. "Yes, I understand," I said as quickly as I could.

"Your son has a rare heart defect called transposition of the great arteries. I know you do not know what that is, but it means his arteries are switched and he is not getting oxygen in his blood," the doctor said. "I don't have a whole lot of time to explain. Your son needs a procedure called a balloon septostomy. This procedure will keep your son alive until he can have open heart surgery. We will go through the artery that runs on the inside of your son's right leg, with a catheter that has a balloon on the end, all the way up to his heart. We will blow the balloon up and pull the catheter out, ripping a hole in his heart. The hole we create will allow some of the blood that has oxygen to mix with the blood that does not have oxygen. There could be complications with this procedure."

She listed the complications to me, and it sounded like she was reading a tongue twister without missing a word, but the only complications I could remember were, "lose his leg," or, "death". My options, as I understood them, were to let them do this procedure and possibly save his life or, to refuse the procedure, and he would die.

The doctor told me, "Speak very clearly and give me your consent when I ask you."

"Okay," I said.

"Do you consent to the balloon septostomy?" she asked.

"Yes," I replied. There was no response after that, no sound of a caring physician cooing into the phone to tell an anxious mother miles away that everything would be alright. There wasn't even any further discussion at all. All I heard was the doctor's phone hanging up.

What had I just done? Had I made the right decision? I knew it had to be the right one if it was going to save his life, and yet I found myself in complete shock once again. It was more than shock; it felt like my whole body, right down to my soul, had been zapped by a lightening rod.

I lay in my bed and stared at my empty belly, the deflated, stretched skin space where my baby used to be. My mind could not grasp the concept that in such a short time my baby had been healthy and safe and with me, but now he was fighting for his life miles and miles away from where I was.

I replayed the entire conversation, trying to slow it down and analyze it since I had not had that opportunity before. But my anxious mind and my grieving heart muddled the whole thing. I wondered if I'd heard the doctor correctly at all – had she really said open heart surgery, or had I imagined those words? I prayed to God and in between prayers, I tried to remember everything the doctor had told me. I even wrote down the conversation on some random flyer I found in a drawer in my room. I wrote it down because I didn't believe what I had heard.

I know there are moments I don't remember about that long, drawn-out night, but I know I didn't fall asleep either. I am sure my mind just shut down from the mass confusion. I even tried again to let myself cry, but knowing at any moment someone could come in and tell me my baby was gone, I decided I would save my tears for later.

It was very early the next morning when I came out of my daze. I had hoped it was all just a bad dream, but the way I felt I knew it wasn't. I got up out of bed and went in to take a bath. Of all the stupid things to cry about, I cried because I wanted a hot bath and I could only get that dumb hospital water lukewarm. It seemed tragic, but in a trivial way. I sat in the tub crying, wishing I could get some stupid hot water. I had been able to stop myself from crying about Manie all night, but there I was crying over bath water the next morning. Then I cried about how stupid I felt by the irony of that. My bath lasted just long enough to cry and wash up and rinse off.

I soon realized that something as meaningless as a hot bath was different. I didn't deserve to have that hot bath, not when my baby was laying somewhere far away without me, suffering. He didn't get a nice soothing bath. If he couldn't know that kind of comfort, how wonderful a nice, hot bath can be, then I was relieved I had only had lukewarm water for myself. I knew I didn't deserve anything that would cause me an ounce of happiness as long as Manie had to suffer. Somehow the lukewarm bath seemed fitting then, and I was glad I had been able to experience some small bit of suffering, especially since Manie was going through so much of his own.

I quickly got dressed and got all my stuff ready to go. Mary showed up and I felt a little relief again. We did not get to say much to each other before Dr. Pranger came in to tell me he signed my release papers and I could go. You know something is really serious when the doctor doesn't make you wait around. Before I left he explained to me what he could about Manie's heart defect. I think he knew that my brain was on overload and was not functioning enough to take anymore explanations or even big words. He said, "Make sure when you're in Iowa City to ask a lot of questions."

Before he left I remember looking at him and thinking, I wish you could go with me. I wanted to beg him, but I knew I couldn't take the rejection of him telling me he couldn't go. I knew he was just as friendly with all his patients, it is just who he is. I am sure the good doctor would hold each patients hand all the way to the end, but it would be impossible. Knowing all that still didn't stop me from wanting to beg for him to go. I was terrified I would get to Iowa City and not understand a word anyone was saying.

I knew going to the new hospital would be much like going to a foreign country without much knowledge of the language. What if I was asked to make decisions and I made the wrong ones? Somebody's life was at stake and not just anybody's life; my own baby's life was hanging in the balance. The decisions I had to make would affect his life forever. I definitely wasn't in the right mind to make any decisions, let alone ones that would determine the rest of another human being's life.

The ride to Iowa City was the longest hour and a half of my life. It felt like I could not get there fast enough. I kept thinking what an unselfish person Mary had been. She had spent all night with Manie and Russell, even though she was supposed to be at work and she has four kids of her own to take care of. On top of everything she had already done, she came and picked me up and took me to Iowa City to be with Manie. How strange it was I didn't feel guilty for asking so much of one person. I knew I should have felt bad that Mary had gone out of her way to help me, but I did not feel bad at all. I just felt lucky and grateful to have someone in my life that cared that much about us.

During the drive to Iowa City Mary and I did not really talk about how Manie was doing. We talked about things like what part of the hospital Manie was in, and what the doctor had told me over the phone the night before. I expressed my disbelief over what was happening. What I wanted to believe was the doctors had made some horrible mistake and they were wrong. I wanted to believe when I got there I could just hold him and give him a kiss and somehow make it all better. These are the hopes of a grieving mother, and they were hardly rationale.

Finally we pulled into the parking garage, got out of the car and began our long journey through the hospital. It didn't seem to matter what part of the hospital we were passing through, it all felt lonely, cold and confusing. As soon as we arrived at the nursery intensive care unit, or NICU as everyone called it, I didn't want to talk to anybody. I just wanted to get to my baby; I just wanted to see Manie with my own eyes. I don't really remember if I actually did talk to anybody, if I did I am certain my mouth was on autopilot and my mind was on him.

I walked into the nursery and was reminded to wash my hands as soon as I entered and then use hand sanitizer to kill anything remaining. The smell of the alcohol from the sanitizer left an unsettling association between sanitized and what was now my new reality. As I prepped to be acceptable to go near Manie, I could see his crib from where I stood. The sanitizer was barely dry on my hands when I started to move towards him. As I walked closer I saw him lying there with his eyes closed and his body swollen. He looked like a different baby than what I had seen the night before. Most notably, he was no longer blue like he had been, but he had more tubes and wires surrounding him. Everything about him was being monitored by machines; his bassinet even had a heat lamp over the top, which would turn on when his body temperature demanded additional warmth.

Underneath his body was a pillow. He lay there on his fluffy, soft cushion, unconscious; they were still keeping him sedated with morphine so he would not feel anything. I sat next to him and touched his little hand. In that moment, my irrational hopes fled and I knew I was not going to be able to kiss Manie and make this all go away. As I stood there looking at my baby fighting for his life the words 'everything happens for a reason' echoed in my mind once again.

I flashed back to when I was 11 years old and I stood at my mother's casket looking at her dead body lying there and knowing I couldn't do anything to bring her back. The pain and emptiness I felt in that moment came rushing back through my veins as if it was fresh and new again. In that very moment it dawned on me that if Mom had not passed away when I was so young, I would never have known the pain of someone dying. If she had left me when I was older, I wouldn't understand what it was to lose so much of myself. If I had not had that horrendous pain stuck in the back of my mind, I would not have been so determined to keep Manie here on this earth. It was in my mother's contract with me to teach me many things in my life and in that moment I understood she had already taught me the most important lesson – because I knew what it felt like to lose someone so important, now faced with the same potential situation again, I wasn't going to let it happen a second time.

Now I knew the reason why my mother suffered and then left me and I was going to use it for everything it was worth. Everything that had already happened with Manie seemed less possible to me than Manie waking up and being perfectly healthy. A miracle had to be possible in my mind for Manie to get through this nightmare. I could not stand the thought of life without him. I had never heard of energy healing before, such as Reiki, and it wouldn't be until years later that I would become familiar with the idea of it. Yet in that moment there with Manie, I laid my hands on him and began to pray that any energy I had be passed to him. I prayed to God and asked that He let my child have whatever strength I had left in my weak body.

I am at a loss of words to explain the feelings I felt in those moments, knowing my energy was transferring to Manie, but I do know it happened and it was real, and strong and powerful.

Real is a term that can mean so many things. Laying my hands on Manie didn't cure him instantly, of course. Manie still had to go through what he needed to, to fulfill his contract and make him Manie. Sometimes miracles don't happen in a way that makes you drop your jaw in awe of some extraordinary event. Sometimes the miracle is in looking back and seeing exactly how life fit together. Sometimes the miracle is in seeing a reason, even in the extremely bad situations in life. There wasn't a machine to measure the energy I was giving to Manie; the miracle was that despite having evidence, I knew I was helping him survive and I believed in something that was completely unseen.

Back in reality, I met so many doctors, student doctors, and nurses within my first couple of hours at the hospital that my head was spinning and cluttered with the words they said. I was so tired and exhausted; I had even forgotten I had just gone through hours of labor. Manie's nurse told me the hospital had rooms for mothers who had babies in the intensive care unit. She told me she would check and see if I could stay in one of the rooms. I didn't care about having a room. Why would I need a room? I did not plan on leaving my baby for even a moment! I was hoping the nurse would forget I was even there and forget about the room.

I was in it for the long haul. I was ready to plant myself in the chair for as long as Manie was laying there in that bassinet. I was just sitting there with Manie, God only knows how long it must have been, probably hours, holding his tiny motionless hand. His nurse told me, "You have to go get some rest and something to eat. You have been here too long."

Russell and Mary had gone home. I realized I couldn't remember them leaving or even saying good bye. I knew I was all alone and the nurse wanted me to leave.

"I am fine here," I replied to the nurse. She wouldn't listen to me though; she wanted me to leave and became very persistent about it. I began to get the feeling I would be dragged out kicking and screaming if I didn't follow her instructions. I looked at the nurse straight in the eyes. "You better take care of my baby," I demanded. She assured me she would.

I jumped down from the tall bar stool-like chair they had given me to sit on. I looked around the room for the first time. I realized Manie and I were not the only ones in the NICU, there were a lot of babies in the intensive care unit. My son, weighing seven and a half pounds, looked like a giant compared to all the other babies weighing just ounces. Some of the babies could fit in the palm of one of my hands. Most of the babies were under what looked like a thin sheet of plastic which was to protect their delicate skin. Just thinking about how I could have been there for hours and not have noticed these tiny precious beings made me lose my breath for a second. After taking one more look at Manie and whispering to him, "I will be right back, I love you," I walked to the hallway.

My feet started to throb in my shoes. I felt sick to my stomach. My ankles were the size of softballs, they had become swollen from letting my short legs dangle while I sat on the stool next to Manie's crib. I started to walk though this huge hospital trying to find my way outside. I was so scared I would get lost. I tried to remember which turn and twist I was supposed to take. Making a mental map of which way I was to go was difficult when all I could think about was leaving Manie there all alone. After about twenty minutes of wandering the maze, which some called a hospital, I made it outside. Across the street I saw a little bus shelter. I crossed the road and thanked God that it was empty. I thanked Him there was a place to sit and keep warm under the heat lamp from the cold March winds. I sat down and I started to cry; this time the tears came with no effort on my part.

I really didn't want to cry in fear someone might come in and ask me what was wrong. If someone had asked me, I don't think I would have known what to say. I was angry beyond normal anger, I was confused, frustrated, weak and just plain sad. I started praying to God and asked Him to keep my baby safe and make him better. I begged God to let me switch places with Manie. I tried to bargain with God and tell Him if He would make this all go away, I would do anything He wanted. I never felt anger towards God or wanted to blame Him. I had to keep my promise to my mom to never blame God. I wanted God on my side; I needed to feel as if God was there protecting Manie.

CHAPTER 5

DEPTHS OF DESPAIR

"The pain you feel today will be the strength you rely on tomorrow."
[Unknown]

The longer I sat in that shelter, the more furious and impatient I grew. Feelings brewed inside me, not positive ones, like poison hidden insidiously inside a venomous snake. I wanted to strike, yet there was no one to be my victim, no one except the one person I had counted on my whole life.

Mothers are supposed to be the one person we can count on to walk by our side, even if only in spirit. My thoughts were jumbled and irrational, and in their midst I settled on a victim. I knew exactly who was going to be the recipient of my wrath. It was my mom! She made me make that stupid promise to never blame God. My Mom let this happen to Manie. I was mad at her for not being physically there to help me and, even worse, I suddenly realized not only was she not there physically, I couldn't feel her spirit around me anymore either. I became even angrier with her because I felt abandoned, once again.

I felt completely alone for the first time in my life. I felt like I was like an unwanted dog, dropped off on a country road and left to fend for myself. Ever since Mom died I had always felt like there was someone there with me. I always knew it was Mom looking over me, watching out for me. As I sat there under the heat lamp I felt nothing, I felt completely alone. I started to yell at Mom in my head. No longer was my mother a sacred being to be cherished, she was just my mom, and she had failed me. I spoke to her for the first time like a daughter would to a mother who was still alive.

"I am so pissed off at you! Why in the hell did you let this happen to my son? Why did you let this happen to me? Why can't you be here with me? Don't you think that I have been through enough?" I said, wanting Mom to appear right there in the shelter before me to explain herself. Then I moved on to threats, telling her I was sick of everything and threatening to give up completely. "It's not fair," I shouted. "I can't do this anymore; I can't be strong for everyone around me, especially when I need someone to be strong for me! Where are you and why aren't you here to walk me through this? I'm giving up, I'm done!"

I desperately wanted someone to feel sorry for me because, for the first time in my life, I would not allow me to be sorry for me. I was not the one fighting for my life, Manie was. I was not the one going through all the pain, Manie was. I felt selfish for even being sad because any pain I had to go through was nothing compared to the physical pain Manie was in. I began to feel regret for my outburst then, and I told Mom, "I am so sorry for yelling at you. Please, please, please Mom, keep my baby safe!"

I told her I knew she understood and I told her I loved her. That is when I realized the reason why I felt so alone and the reason I didn't feel her with me anymore was because she found someone who needed her more than I did. My mom was with her grandson, keeping him safe. I didn't feel her presence around me because she was with him, the one person who needed her protection more than I did in that moment. I felt selfish for expecting her to take care of me, and I felt regret for insisting that she be around me again.

I made my way back to inside the hospital, wanting to get back to Manie as soon as possible. My head was dizzy and my stomach was churning though, and progress towards the NICU was slow. I couldn't see anything in front of me and, for a moment, I did not even know where I was. My worst fear was passing out somewhere in the hospital and not making it back to the nursery to see Manie and hold his little hand. I leaned on the wall for a minute, taking deep breaths, and then started walking slowly again as the walls and the floors began to swirl around me.

I know I made it back to the nursery, but I don't know how. I don't remember walking or even how I knew where to go. My brain was foggy and swimming in and out of consciousness. I was not even sure what was real anymore.

Being back with Manie I felt it, I wasn't alone. There it was – that feeling of having Mom with me, the very same feeling I had missed outside. My mom was back. I said to Mom in my head, "Thank you for being here when I could not; I missed you."

I had planned to just sit there with Manie and watch his every breath. Of course the nurse was not going to let that happen. She reminded me of the room the hospital had available. She began to go through a list of rules if I was to utilize the room. In a scolding voice she said, "The room is just for you no one else." Although I was not a patient, I had to sign in and out of my room. She pointed me towards the direction of the door and told me, "Go lay down for a while."

I felt as if I was being kicked me out of the intensive care unit again. The normal me, the one with the sassy mouth who says what she feels, the one with the mouth that gets her in trouble and would have instinctively said, "I'm not going! He is my baby and I will be with him if I want!" wasn't on duty that day. I knew if I wanted to be with Manie I had to listen to the nurse. Another nurse escorted me to my room, which was a turn to the left down the long hall and two more turns to the left off the NICU where Manie was. I made another mental map in my mind so I would not forget where to go when I wanted to get back, which I was positive would be sooner rather than later.

The nurse that directed me was somewhat cold. I sensed she had an attitude toward me, and probably everyone else she had ever come in contact with. Her attitude made me well aware that it was a big hassle to help me and she should be doing better things with her time.

"You are not allowed to have anyone back in your room, especially men," the nurse said in a sharp tone. The way that haggard nurse said it made me feel like I had done something wrong. In hindsight, I wondered, did she really think I was going to have men back in my room? The last thing on my mind, knowing my baby was suffering in the NICU, was a man. The last thing any woman thinks about after having a baby is a man or wanting one around her for the purpose of what the nurse was suggesting. Her suggestion was preposterous and offensive.

The room was your typical, outdated hospital room with two beds, a TV and a bathroom. The nurse then asked me, "Are you planning on breastfeeding?"

"I did before I had him, but I am not sure if I still can since he was not going to get anything to eat until after his surgery," I replied.

The nurse gave me a weird look with her ugly wrinkled face as if I was stupid for even thinking I could not nurse my baby still. She handed me a breast pump, attachments, some labels and some baggies and told me, "The breast pump machines are in this room here." She pointed with her wicked, boney, crooked looking finger to a closet along our path.

Then she grabbed a huge, ancient dinosaur of a machine from the closet. It was on a long metal post which had wheels at the bottom. The nurse clumsily dragged the machine along as we walked to my room.

Once we reached my room the nurse parked the machine in front of what was now my bed and said, "You won't get any milk the first few times, but you had better start pumping. The freezer to store your milk is down the hall."

Boy, was that the last thing on my mind at that time. The lady left and there I was all alone again. This time I was not as scared to be alone because I knew at least someone who loved and cared for Manie was with him; my mom. There are some things your mind will just allow you to believe when you are on the edge of insanity and sanity.

I sat down on my hospital bed and looked at my ankles; they were getting bigger and my shoes were so tight my ankles folded over the tops of my shoes. As good as it would have felt, I did not bother to take my shoes off. I knew if I did I would not be able to force my feet back in. I looked over at the table and sitting there was a phone. I felt some relief knowing that I could call home and talk to Russell. I could not even remember the last time I had spoken to him. Russell and I had not had a chance to even discuss what was happening yet. I called home, just wanting to talk to someone. I wanted someone to know I was scared and lonely. Russell got mad at me because he was not in the mood to talk; all he wanted to do was sleep. He didn't say hardly anything at all. He was short with his answers and didn't ask how anyone or anything was. I felt so disappointed and alienated.

I knew it would make me feel better to know that at least my other children were doing fine. I called to check on them. Haley and Alex had been at their grandmother's house. They didn't know much about what happened other than that their new baby brother was sick. Grif had been with Russell's mom and I was happy he was doing well and wasn't old enough to even know what was going on. My phone calls with them were short, but made me feel a little better if even just for a few moments.

Once off the phone I sat there trying to remember what the doctors had told me. I tried to piece together the bits of information I could recall. I wanted to make sense out of everything so I could try to understand what was happening to my little guy. I felt like everything was a big test, but I did not have any books or notes to study from. It may sound wrong, but I took comfort in the fact that I at least knew my whole world was crashing down around me and I could not do anything about it. This kind of logic was my new world. It was a world of chaos and insanity. Time seem to stand still, though all I wanted was for it all to be over with and to be home with my baby.

I used the breast pump to try to pass a little time and to help me forget about my legs and feet and how bad they hurt. At last something was going right and I was actually able to get a couple of ounces of breast milk. I wanted to go and wave those tiny couple of ounces in the face of the nurse who told me I would not get any milk my first few times, but I could not stand even looking at her horrible, mean face again.

I stood up from sitting on my bed, I could feel my toes stuffed and squishing together in my shoes. The intensity of the aches and pains in my feet and legs caused me to limp as I walked down the hall to the freezer and made my deposit. I hobbled back to my room, hanging on the hand rail that ran alongside the wall. There was a great relief when I reached my bed. I turned the TV on and started to watch. No matter what channel I turned to, everything seemed so meaningless and just plain dumb. Flipping through the channels made me realize how even the simplest things had changed. I thought about how many times I have thought something was so bad and I felt the world was ending, and now anything I have ever gone through could not compare to what Manie was going through, or the complete and total despair that I felt. I finally feel asleep that night for about an hour and a half, partially reclined and slouched over on the tiny bed. I can only imagine I looked much like a drunk person who passes out without any thought to comfort.

When I woke, I knew for sure it had to all be a bad dream. I laid there for a couple of minutes convincing myself if I opened my eyes I would be home and everything would be normal. When I finally worked up the courage to open my eyes, devastation washed over me once again. I saw the hospital room that haunted me in my nightmare. Instead of my nightmare happening when I closed my eyes, it existed when they were wide open. Every awful feeling I had felt since Manie had been born had manifested itself onto my physical body. Every inch of me was exhausted and sore. It was a pain that, if under different circumstances, would have made me wonder if I was dying. And yet, I stood up and took a few steps anyway, unable even then to completely submit to the pain and stay in bed and succumb to it. I was determined to see Manie.

I really didn't care that I was in so much pain. I cried about it anyways. I cried because I wondered why, through all this, something as stupid as my pain had to matter. Then I realized my pain did not matter at all, I was just looking for a reason to cry again. My tears had built up inside me like water trapped in a hose that had a kink. Any excuse to cry was like puncturing that hose just a little bit and relieving some of the pressure. I cried just enough to let some of the pain escape, but not enough to make it look like I had been crying. The last thing I wanted was for anyone to ask me how I was feeling or have sympathy towards me. I knew if someone did, I would start crying and not be able to stop.

I got out of bed and felt that dizzy, buzzed feeling you get when you have not had enough sleep. I knew I was going to have to do a lot of pretending if I was going to make everyone think I was well rested. I pulled my long hair back into a ponytail so I would not have to bother with brushing it. I changed into the clothes I had brought with me from the other hospital and I tried as hard as I could to look normal, or at least human. I walked down to the nurse's station to sign out and asked if I could have some Ibuprofen for the pain in my legs and feet.

It was that same evil looking nurse again. She sat behind her desk, just looking at me like I was an idiot. The warden told me she could not give me anything because I wasn't a patient. In a very robotic and calm manner I explained my situation to the nurse, but she did not extend any compassion for my problems. "The pharmacy will open in a few hours; you could get some from there," she said, and continued to shuffle papers around her desk. I signed myself out and walked away from the snarling beast, and sucked back my tears.

I headed down the hall to the NICU. I knew if I could just see Manie again I would be alright. As I entered the room I saw Manie's nurse tending to him. I asked how he was doing and I got a whole bunch of medical mumbo jumbo which I'm sure was used on purpose to confuse me and make me feel like it was the nurse who was in control, not me. I got the feeling the nurse was trying to prove to me how much smarter than me she was. I nodded my head up and down as I pretended to know what she was talking about and started asking questions. Maybe I was coming off as stupid or the nurse thought I had lost my mind. She just kind of looked at me as if I was pestering her.

That was my first experience with the game these nurses played which I like to call "the run around". I had no tolerance for a nurse who didn't want to tell me she just didn't know if my baby was going to make it or not. Why couldn't they just be honest, and human, with me?

CHAPTER 6

FORCED AWAY

"God's grace is painted on the canvas of despair. [T. D. Jakes]

I have the utmost respect for nurses, I really do, and yet I can't help but wonder at the specialized language and communication skills used by the NICU nurses in Manie's hospital. I can only describe it as a mixture between evasive, distant, and B.S. It didn't matter who I asked questions of, they all spewed the same generic format at me. I realized now the confusing medical talk was just the nurses' way of pacifying my annoying need to know more about my son's condition, as if by confusing me they could make me go away. After a while they just started telling me I would have to wait to talk to the doctor, who never seemed to be around.

If they weren't answering my questions with medical jargon straight from their nursing school textbooks, they were trying to get rid of me in other ways, or so it felt. I remember one particular nurse who made it a point to tell me, "Get some sleep," every time she came near Manie. Though I repeatedly responded with, "I'm okay; I already did," it didn't stop her from repeating herself a half hour later.

I wanted answers, and in the absence of those, I wanted to sit and stare at my baby and touch him to reassure myself he was still alive. As each minute passed by my arms ached from the feeling of emptiness caused by not being able to hold and comfort Manie.

After getting some rest, I sat with Manie from 2:00 a.m. until 8:00

a.m. Then I was once again forced from my chair, which I had now declared the only place I belonged in this world, and made to leave the nursery.

I found a phone sitting in a waiting room near the NICU, so I called Russell again. I wanted to tell him how horrible I felt, how bad things had been that night and how upset I was, but the only words I could get out were, "Get up here now!" When I hung up the phone I felt mad at Russell because he went home and he slept in our bed. My anger was interrupted by someone putting money into the vending machine and it reminded me that I could not remember the last time I had eaten. Food felt trivial somehow, and even if it hadn't, I had no money anyway. Even if I had been hungry and had some money to buy food, I still don't think I would have eaten; leaving Manie's side to eat seemed a waste of the time I could be spending with him. For the first time in my life, food wasn't a problem.

I dismissed thoughts of food then and headed back into the NICU. The nurse was getting ready to clean out Manie's breathing tube and I stood there and observed the horrible, but necessary, task. I hated the fact that Manie needed a breathing tube, though I understood why it was necessary. I looked at the tube, how it jabbed its way down his tiny throat, and was overcome by the feeling of wanting to grab the nurse's hand and shove that tube down her throat in an attempt to stop her from torturing my son. Her carelessness as she cleaned out the tube was unsettling. She may as well have been sweeping a kitchen floor or pumping gas, or any other routine chore that did not demand tenderness or gentleness. I know she had probably done this a thousand times before, but Manie had already been through so much; couldn't she be even a little sympathetic?

Shortly after the cleaning, and with me having resumed my perch at Manie's bedside, the doctor finally showed up to make his rounds. I braced myself, ready for his updates and eager for them as well.

The doctor threw a lot of words at me, but the only thing I could hear was, "As soon as Manie is stable enough we will be doing the open heart surgery. It will have to be in the next few days."

It was a relief to talk to the doctor, but the words "open heart surgery" stunned me like a Taser to the forehead. It sent the thoughts coming from an already fried brain to that solitary place I was starting to become way too familiar with, a place filled with anxiety and angst. How do you even react to being told something so horrible? How exactly are you supposed to feel about your newborn baby going through something as risky as open heart surgery? On one hand it would save his life and, on the other hand, it could take his life. My imagination flooded my mind with their rendition of how open heart surgery might look, and took over my mind without my permission.

I pictured taking home a baby with stitches down the middle of his chest. I pictured the scar that would be left forever as a reminder of this time in our lives. My heart sank as I thought about my life without Manie if surgery didn't go well. Worst of all, I pictured all the pain in his life he would have to feel. I felt wrong and horrible for thinking about any of it. I felt like there was something wrong with me because my imagination was running away with me. I felt selfish for wanting to get it all over with. I felt guilty because I could not take care of the other kids.

Tortured by my own thoughts, I had to constantly remind myself to stop thinking. The reminder stuck for about ten seconds, and then my head was immersed in my fears and guilt all over again. And yet thinking was the only thing I could do when I sat there alone with Manie, watching him. Most of my thinking was done in the form of prayers. Begging and praying are all the same thing when you do it the way I did. When I wasn't praying, I was riding tidal waves of anxiety. Without anyone or anything to distract me from myself, I was driving myself insane with "what if" scenarios that were holding me hostage.

Just when I could not stand to be alone with my thoughts another second, Russell finally showed up. It had only been a little over a day since I had last seen him, but it felt like he had been gone for years.

He stayed with me by Manie's bedside, though our conversation was strained and difficult. After a couple of hours, he informed we that we needed to go home so we could figure out "what we are going to do." With not much money and three other kids to take care of, we really were lost. He could not have known how poorly timed his statement was. A strong sense of hatred built up inside me and I thought, are you nuts? You want me to leave my baby and go home?

Home was an hour and a half away from Manie. The nurses were urging me to go home and rest. Everyone was against me and I was weak and tired. How dare they pick on me when I needed to be there for Manie and when we had gone through so much! My body was sore and my feet were going to explode at the ankles from being so swollen. They were all cold hearted and thoughtless, I felt. All I knew was the last time I had left someone in the hospital, she died. I was expected to do it again? The nurses were teaming up with Russell then and they all nagged at me until I was completely broken down.

There was no way around it, ultimately. I had to go; I could not keep up the fight. My body was completely spent of all energy. I told Russell. "I am going home to get my clothes and that's it. I'm coming back here right away."

With those words spoken, the tension between myself and Russell and the nurses began to subside. It seemed to make everyone's day that I was so broken and weak I couldn't fight back anymore. The nurses assured me they would take care of Manie and contact me if there were any problems. They let me know I could call and check on him anytime I wanted. No one but me was taking this as seriously as they should be; no one could see things from my point of view, because I was the mother of a baby with a heart defect. In truth, Manie and

I were the same and, unlike anyone else in that room, we were both suffering from broken hearts.

The ride home was horrible. Going home without Manie felt egregious; it felt void of common sense or any sense at all. In my mind, I was the worst mother on the face of the earth – the weakest and the least helpful and, on top of it, I was running away. By the time I got home, I was no longer mad at Russell or the nurses; rather, I was furious with myself. I was mad at myself for leaving and I was pissed off at the entire situation.

I felt like a wild animal trapped in a cage. I wanted to panic at times and when I did, I could not breathe. The only thing that made me feel human was being around my other children and being able to see them healthy.

After spending some time with my kids I went to take a bath and even questioned if I deserved one. Why should I feel good at all if Manie had to suffer there at that hospital all alone? I told myself, "You will get in, get cleaned up, and then get right out."

While in the tub I looked down at my belly. It was empty. I could not feel my baby move anymore. The last time I had taken a bath in this bath tub, I was pregnant. The last time I left this house, I was still pregnant. I just wanted to go back in time, back to months ago when I first learned of being pregnant, back to a time when it seemed I would be pregnant forever, and I wanted to stay there. Of course there was no going back now, but I also could not see the end to all of this chaos. I looked backwards with longing and forward with anxiety, and my present moment was tortured. Where was the way out?

I got out of the tub, wrapped up in my towel and went to lie down on my bed. I stared at the bassinet where Manie should be and I started to cry. I was in the comfort of my home where I didn't have to worry about holding back the tears.

Although I had people around me, I was alone, just like Manie. I wanted to leave and go be with him, but I knew I had things to take care of first. I wanted Russell to comfort me, but he just left me alone. I wanted to sleep, but I wanted to spend time with my other children more. I knew they needed me to explain to them exactly what was happening to their baby brother. What a God awful moment it was trying to explain to two little girls that their new baby brother was fighting for his life in another town. Thankfully, I had become a master at not crying in front of people. Looking at their innocent little faces made it hard to hold back the tears though, so I said just enough and moved on to other subjects instead, like what they had been doing at their grandma's house.

I spent a little time with the kids before I knew I would have to go again. I had only been home a few hours before I told Russell I had to go back. He really didn't want to talk about it, but I did. I nagged at him the way he and the nurses had nagged at me to leave the hospital. He was persistent that he wasn't going to take me back that day and he was not going to help make it possible for me to go back. I called and checked on Manie so many times and I didn't even care if I was annoying. I felt absolutely horrible for not being there every second of the day.

Late that night when everything was quiet and the kids were sleeping, I laid in my bed, hugged a pillow, and pretended it was Manie. I could not escape the loneliness and desperation I felt, so I cried myself to sleep.

I woke the next morning barely able to open my swollen eyes. I rolled my tired and weary body out of bed and tried to at least make myself presentable enough to go out into public. I looked in the mirror at my sad face; I did not really care how I looked and I figured it was fitting somehow to look as horrible as I felt. I looked down at my ankles, noticing they were still swollen and painful.

I made my way to see what everyone else was doing. The kids were still sleeping and I found Russell downstairs sitting in the living room. He told me right away he had come down with a sore throat. The last thing we needed right now was to get sick! What if Russell didn't get to see Manie before his surgery? I decided to call Dr. Pranger to look at my ankles and Russell's throat before we went back to the hospital. I was told not to sit for too long and Russell was told he was fine, but to make sure he wore a mask if he went in to see Manie.

When we arrived back home, I could see our answering machine was completely full of messages. Quickly I played them, hoping to God there wasn't something wrong with Manie. Most of the messages were from friends and telemarketers. There were a couple of urgent messages from a woman at the social security office. Knowing she had tried to contact me while I was at the hospital, I decided her message would be the only one I would bother to return. It was a rushed attempt to complete all my tasks so I could get back to Manie as soon as I could.

The woman told me she wanted me to come down right away to get social security for Manie.

"Social security? He can get disability payments, how is that?" I questioned.

"He has a disabled," the woman on the phone said.

That was the first time I had come face-to-face with the fact that my son had a disability. Disabled is such a harsh word. It means you are not able to do some things and we were, all of us, unsure at that time whether Manie would even live, let alone what things he would and would not be able to do like "normal" people. I wondered what things Manie would not be able to do in his life. What would the future be like for him if he could not do things that he wanted to do?

The woman on the phone scheduled an appointment for me right away.

The Social Security office was right down the road from our house, so it only took me and Russell a couple of minutes to get there. We were in the waiting room long enough for me to look around and think about how much I needed to leave so I could get back to Manie. It was awful sitting there among strangers who had no idea what we had just gone through, and were still going through.

The lady at the Social Security office was pleasant. She knew her job well and I could tell she had been working for the Social Security office for years. She projected her experience onto our situation though, acting as if we had been the parents of a "disabled" child forever and should be used to the process, though we weren't. It was all very new to us. That day was the first time I had to try to explain to someone what "disability" my son was born with. Since the doctors and nurses had been so difficult to understand, speaking in overly-complicated medical phrases I struggled to understand, I wasn't entirely sure how I would be able to relay the details of his condition to the woman. Luckily the woman had papers sent to her from the hospital, so I did not have to explain everything completely to her.

The woman informed us that we should be able to collect SSI for Manie, and we would receive a decision in thirty days. The last thing I cared about was money, but I knew it would help make Manie's life better. Who knew what kind of specialty devices he would need later on?

Russell and I went back home. I was done with all my appointments and had completed each meaningless task that needed to be taken care of. I wanted to go back to be with Manie, though I was becoming panicked with anxiety about how I was going to get back to Iowa City. We weren't just broke, we were downright poor. We were barely scraping by as it was, though we had the bills covered as long as Russell kept working. It wasn't a matter of trying to figure out how I was going to go be with Manie in Iowa City, it was a matter of how fast I was going to figure it out. There were only two answers to my dilemma: I either walked or I found a way to get there by car to be with him, and Russell couldn't be counted on to drive me there, especially since he had to work. Haley and Alex were going to stay at their grandma's house and Grif was just going to have to come with me.

The doctors had given us no clue as to how long Manie would be at the hospital, so I didn't know how long I would have to be away from home, and I didn't care. I would have spent a lifetime waiting there in the hospital next to him if that was how long it took.

I was becoming irritated at Russell's lack of concern about how we were going to pull this off. I knew his point of view was that if he did not think about it, then it was not happening. With each second that passed, I became more and more irritated at his successful attempts to ignore our situation. Finally I yelled at him, "We have to figure this out now and no matter how much you want to pretend this isn't happening, it is! And it is not going to figure itself out!"

I insisted that if he did not help me find a way, I was going to find my own way to Manie's side.

"You can stay here, I don't even care. Just stay home if that's what you want; stay here and pretend this isn't happening!" I was furious and beyond disbelief that he could continue ignoring his son and his son's medical needs.

In reply he just kept telling me, "I don't know what to do."

It was baffling, really. Wasn't his excuse to get me to come home that we needed to figure this out? Now he was telling me he didn't know what to do and refused to help me.

Just when I thought all hope was lost, I hid myself in the bedroom and used all the energy I had left to begged God to help me.

"God please, I have to be with Manie," I said, with all the passion I was holding in my heart.

God sent me an answer. Just minutes after I had prayed, Russell's mom came over and told us to pack our things. We were going to Iowa City to stay, she told us, at least until Manie had his heart surgery. As she took charge and mobilized all of us for the trip, an unfamiliar sensation crept over me. It was strange and unexpected, and completely unfamiliar, to feel myself smiling. I had not smiled since the first time I saw Manie when he was born. And then a wave of worry swept back over me once again, and the smile quickly escaped.

I was worried once more, though my anxiety was starting to lose its edge. In that moment, it was as if an angel put their arms around me and hugged me close. Relief washed over me and I did not care about bills and how we were going to pay them, or anything else for that matter. I knew I was going to miss Haley and Alex, but I knew they would be okay at their grandma's house. Somehow I trusted then that everything would be okay. I stopped worrying about anything beyond the moment. It was spring break and they would have fun being at their grandma's. The only thing I was concerned with was Manie living and being okay, and I knew everything else would work itself out. I wouldn't accept any other life script.

CHAPTER 7

WAITING FOR LIFE

"Hope anchors the soul." [Hebrews 6:19]

Russell, his mom, Grif and I made it back to Iowa City. Russell's mom booked a cheap hotel room right near the hospital and then we went to see Manie. I was so excited to see him!

We walked into the NICU and there he was, laying exactly the way he was when I left him, still fighting for his life. I felt energy come rushing back into my body as soon as I saw him. I never wanted to leave him like that ever again. I belonged by his side and I felt a renewed determination to not let anyone force me away from him again.

Over the next few days I would find out what it meant to have a child with a rare heart defect. The worry, praying and waiting would have driven me mad if I didn't have my focus set on Manie being in my arms, smiling and healthy. I envisioned it in my mind and held on to this image for dear life, as if by focusing on it wholly I could bring it into being.

Despite all the stress I was able to keep my breast milk supply up and save it for when he would be able to eat. The exhausting task of living out a hotel room and a hospital started to become routine. We would wake early in the morning, go to the hospital and take turns watching Grif in the waiting room while the other one of us was with Manie. When it was my turn, I would bring Grif in to sit with Manie and me. Grif would talk to his baby brother in his baby talk and gently hold his little hand. Whenever I saw the two of them together I thought about a day when they would be old enough to play together and maybe even get into a little mischief. I longed for that day to come, quickly.

Everyday seemed to bring never-ending worry and wondering, though. No one ever seemed to have any answers as to when Manie would get his surgery. Most of the nurses were cocky and always rushed, yet they seemed to find time to joke around with their fellow colleagues when back at the nurse's station. At times it was all I could do to hold my tongue. I used the skill I had learned years ago, with my sister, to keep my mouth quiet in extreme circumstances. My motivation for zipping my lips was reminding myself these were the people taking care of my child.

One of those incidents is easy for me to recall because I surprised myself by the extent of my restraint. On the fourth day of being there, one of the nurses scolded me because I was gently rubbing Manie's little leg.

"Don't touch him, it will feel irritating to him," she barked. I could not believe how idiotic she sounded. When, in the whole history of time, has a newborn baby every felt irritated by the comfort of his mother's touch? I ignored her comment and kept touching him.

She barked at me again.

"It's the morphine he's on, that's what will cause him to feel irritated by your touch," she said, as if thinking this additional explanation would help me somehow, or make her look like more of an expert in my eyes, one of the two.

There were no indications of him being uncomfortable. He was unconscious and even if he were awake, which didn't happen very often, I am sure he would find the sound of her ignorant voice more irritating then my touch.

Manie was so heavily medicated he really only woke a couple of times. The times he woke he opened his eyes about half way just for a second. I was excited to see life in him for once. At the same time I didn't want him awake to feel any pain. When he did wake he would try to cry, but all you could hear was the hollowed sound of air going in and out of the air tube. When he tried to cry it was due to the nurse cleaning out his breathing tube. Most of the nurses cleaned out the tube carelessly, as if they were brain dead or their minds had shut off. I continued to be shocked and amazed by the lack of empathy I witnessed from the nurses towards their tiny, helpless patients.

Amongst the all of the cold and careless rocks who had been assigned to tend to Manie, there was a diamond, a nurse named Hope. I found her aptly named. She was older than most of the nurses we had been dealing with, and she talked to me like she knew me. She treated me like I was a mother whose newborn baby was lying there suffering. There were little things she did, like let me take his temperature, change his diaper and rub lotion on him (his skin was peeling off in sheets from drying out under the heat lamp) which made me feel like a partner in my tiny son's care. She made me feel useful, which was something I desperately needed in a time when I felt so worthless.

Hope was an angel and her name was fitting name for someone so kind. Just like that, after only one shift, she was gone. I missed her terribly, but that one shift she worked was enough to give me the hope I needed; because of Hope, I felt justified in expecting the same kindness from the other nurses.

I sat next to Manie one afternoon counting the IV, lines that were connected to him. One, two, three… I continued to count until I made it up to sixteen. It felt as if my mind was blocked, I couldn't count any higher. I know there were way more than sixteen, but I don't think I really wanted to know exactly how many there were. Looking up I could see all the machines which helped keep Manie alive. The rhythmic low humming sound of the machines became comforting because to me it meant life.

The days crept by slowly, one after the next, after the next. Even Grif's bout of motion sickness became part of our strange routine. Grif would throw up on the ride over to the hospital and then again when we stepped into the elevator on the first floor of the hospital, on the way to the NICU. He was just a couple months shy of his second birthday, he had no clue what was going on. He was so little, but this was our new life; and each day, without fail, he would get sick. He had no choice about it thought; like the rest of us, he simply had to hang in there.

Russell's dad brought Haley and Alex up so they could see their baby brother. I wanted them to be with him just for a little bit before the day of surgery came. I know they did not realize things were so serious until they saw him with their own eyes. It was a hard thing for anyone to look at, let alone a child. It had to happen though. They had to see their little brother just in case. I begged my sister Cindy to come to see Manie. She didn't want to at first, but eventually I was able to talk her into it. I don't know why I thought it was important to force her to be there, but it had to be important to someone and it distracted me from the endless waiting.

We waited for what seemed like a lifetime to hear the news that the doctors had finally decided Manie was ready for surgery. In actuality, though it seemed like forever, he was only eight days old. Still, it was wonderful to hear that we were about to begin making progress in getting Manie the surgery he needed.

However, a couple of days before his surgery, we got really bad news. The procedure they had done to save his life when he first arrived, the procedure I agreed to and said "yes" to on the phone, caused damage to the artery in Manie's leg. The catheter tube they had to use on him for the balloon septostomy was not the right size. They had used a tube that was meant for a baby the age of a year or older.

"Because of the damage to the artery, Manie could lose his right leg," one of the doctors explained to Russell and me.

The next morning we came in and noticed Manie had a black X written in marker on his right foot. We were told it showed where they had last found a pulse, and it also represented which leg would be amputated if they couldn't bring it back to life. I watched hour after hour as they checked for a pulse in his leg and foot and could not find one. My heart sank into my stomach every time they would check and would find nothing.

Through my close observation over that time, I saw his foot turn from a nice peach to blue, and then to purple; then it started to swell. It was bad enough Manie had to have open heart surgery, now it seemed he would lose his leg too! He would wake up and his leg would be gone. Why did this baby have to have such a horrible beginning?

Thoughts of Manie growing up without his leg ran through my mind constantly. How can life be so unfair to one baby, but yet more than fair to others? I did not understand why they could not have just had the proper equipment to use on Manie. I found myself begging to God again.

"God please do not let this happen to Manie. I know You will make him better, please just let him live through his surgery and let him keep his leg."

The moments I spent with Manie were spent with my hands on his leg, praying that prayer a million times. I breathed all my energy into accepting that Manie and his leg would be fine. And at the end of the day when I had to leave to go back to the hotel room, I continued to pray.

The next day the doctors told us they were putting Manie on a blood thinner in preparation for the surgery. My prayer for his leg to be saved was answered – they had found a pulse shortly after putting him on the medication! They decided he could keep his leg!

As each moment drew us closer to the big event, the NICU became increasingly busy with preparations for the surgery. It seemed like every five minutes someone different was talking to me, from doctors to nurses, anesthesiologists and more nurses. They all had questions for me and wanted to know if I had questions for them. These people, who had once been so scarce that I questioned their very existence, were surrounding me constantly now.

The doctor that would do the actual open heart surgery came in and explained to me some of the things that would happen during the procedure.

"Manie's heart is about the size of a walnut," he said. "His arteries are about half the size of the lead in a pencil."

I had never thought about the size of Manie's heart, and it did nothing to calm my nerves. I was more nervous than ever, after hearing that. His heart was so tiny that my mind couldn't comprehend how the doctor would be able to fix it.

He also told me, "If Manie had been born just a few years before, he probably would have died. Now, with the advances we have in medicine, he has a ninety percent chance of living."

Was that supposed to make me feel better? I kept telling myself I would only accept Manie being fine and something bad happening to Manie was not an option. I have been known to be a little bull-headed and I felt now was a good time to utilize that aspect of my personality.

Manie was moved to a different nursery. It was a nursery for babies who were recovering from surgery. It was a lot like the NICU but instead of having a tiny bassinet, Manie was going to be in a hospital crib. There was a rocking chair for people who came to visit him instead of just a tall stool to sit on. The other babies were still all in the same room, but this time they were Manie's size or bigger. All of the other babies in the new nursery had already had their surgery. Each one had been in there for something different.

I looked at the little baby girl whose crib was next to Manie's. She looked so innocent and helpless laying there. No one was around to comfort her and it made me think of all the times that I had left Manie.

Shortly after arriving in the recovery nursery, a middle-aged woman with shoulder length, straight, blonde hair dressed in a long white lab coat came in.

"Have you held your baby yet?" she asked me.

I looked into her eyes and said, "No."

She looked back into my eyes and said, "Well you need to."

My heart began to race. This lady had better be serious! For the first time I felt like someone cared, someone knew my pain. The doctor looked at the nurse and gave her a nod. The nurse seemed to be irritated at the thought of me holding my own baby. It would mean she would have to maneuver wires and tubes just to let me hold him, but I didn't care. I didn't let her crisp attitude sour me. I was going to hold my baby!

Then the doctor asked where Manie's father was. "Dad needs to hold baby too," she said.

"I will get him right away!" I replied. Before I raced off to find Russell, I spoke to her again, from a place deep in my heart. Grabbing her hand, I said, "Thank you. Thank you so, so much!"

She smiled, but said nothing as I rushed off. I don't think that I had to tell her how thankful I was because she somehow already knew.

I found Russell in the lounge down the hall and told him, "We are going to hold Manie!"

I don't think he believed me at first, or maybe he was nervous about holding Manie, because he just stood there for a second or two, stunned.

"Come on!" I yelled. "Before they change their mind!"

Russell and I arrived back at Manie's bedside and the nurse had already started to move wires around. She instructed me to sit in the big rocking chair right next to Manie's bed. The nurse told me I would have to just hold him on the pillow he was on, so as not to disturb him too much. The last thing I wanted to do was cause Manie any discomfort, so I didn't care if there was a pillow between us; I just wanted my baby in my arms.

The nurse slowly moved Manie from his bed. As she came towards me I took a deep breath; then I held it. Christmas, my birthday, the Fourth of July and all other holidays wrapped into one still could not describe the feeling I got when I held Manie on that day! I never wanted to move again. The next twenty minutes were pure, unwavering bliss, coming from some magical place I never knew could exist in this world or any other. That moment when I was allowed to hold him was the beginning of the rest of my life. My eyes were opened and the heavens shined down on me. I knew I would never see any moment the same way again. My entire perspective on life changed in that moment.

I did not want to hand Manie over, but I thought it was only fair to let Russell share this wonderful feeling. I maneuvered my way past the wires, the tubes, and the nurse as she hovered Manie over my lap. Russell then moved his way into the chair so he could hold Manie. I could tell it was the first time any of this was real for him. I know he held back the tears as he sat there with Manie in his arms. Up until this point I knew Russell had hoped, as I had, that it was all just a nightmare. As I watched Russell hold Manie, the experience felt like a daydream. He and I even had a normal conversation. We were just two normal parents having a normal conversation while holding our baby. When we were done I wondered why the doctor let us hold him. Was it because she was a really nice doctor who cared that we had never held our baby? Or was it because this might be the one and only time we could hold Manie before something bad might happen?

It made me sick to think that that might have been the reason, that it would be our last time to hold him, but then I told myself not to care because, for whatever reason, I had gotten to hold Manie even once, and nothing else mattered. What mattered was holding him and feeling what it was like and knowing I was going to feel it again. Holding Manie felt like an addiction to me. I craved it so bad I couldn't think of anything else.

When Manie was back in his crib, everything settled down. Quickly life got back to what we had been considering normal. I knew things had changed though, and they were going to change even more the following day when Manie had his surgery. It was all just a matter of time now. I hung onto the memory of what it was like to hold Manie in my arms. The warmth and sanity I felt while doing so was enough to get me through the rest of the day and the night.

CHAPTER 8

FEELING CRAZY

"Where hope grows, miracles blossom." [Elna Rae]

My mind and my heart the night before Manie's open heart surgery were busy places and I was grateful no one had visibility into all I was thinking. If they had, I'm sure I would have been committed to a mental institution. I wouldn't doubt that just one peek inside my mind by an outsider would have driven them mad; I was, after all, driving myself mad. There was a raucous, tumultuous mixture of confusion, emotional ups and downs, and a tug-of-war between accepting my reality and denying it.

Specifically, I beat myself up because Manie had to go through this, though I also wasn't quite sure there was anything I could have done to prevent it. I was mad at myself for being happy that he was finally going to have the surgery when it meant his tiny body was about to be subjected to such a delicate, invasive, risky procedure. I was disgusted with myself that I wouldn't be by his side, even though there was nothing I could do to change that.

The thoughts whirling through my head would not stop, even when I tried to force them into silence. Mostly I was terrified Manie would die during his surgery. The sadness of this thought and the fear associated with it transformed into something debilitating: I was furious at myself for even allowing that thought into my head, even for a second.

I felt alone because no one could understand what I was going through, not even his father. I prayed as hard as I could, but knew I would never feel it would be enough. The thoughts just kept going round and round. I could take a hundred years of trying to explain those feeling I had and I still would not be able to describe them enough to make someone understand.

Needless to say, I did not sleep even one wink that night. I laid in bed thinking and listening to Grif and Russell breathing. It was pointless to even attempt to close my eyes.

When my torturous night ended and the sun arose, it was March, 17, 2004, St. Patty's Day. Our little man, with a pinch of Irish from his father's side of the family, was set to have his surgery. When morning came I realized time goes on whether you want it to or not, though I had no control over how fast it crawled or anyway to speed up and skip the day so we could arrive sooner at the other side of his surgery, his recovery, and his (hopefully) trip home.

As I walked into the hospital I had the strangest feeling that this might be the last time I made the trek through these corridors to see Manie. I found myself in that place again where I had to grapple with my fears to arrive back again at knowing Manie not living through this could not be an option. But it was a moment-to-moment battle to stay hopeful, and I knew it would only be a matter of minutes before I was once again grappling with myself.

In between arguing with myself about my predictions for an outcome I could not foresee, I thought about Manie's future. I knew that, regardless of the surgery's outcome, Manie would never be the same again, and that was the only thing I could be sure of. I wondered how much pain he would be in after the surgery, and grieved that I would not be able to discern his levels or types of pain because he couldn't talk to me. How was I going to explain to Manie that I knew he was hurting, but someday the pain would not be so bad? How was I going to explain to him it would all be worth it to hang in there and fight for life? The only thing Manie had ever known up to this point in his life on earth was pain. Would it be worth it to him to fight for life? How was I going to explain it to Manie so he would fight to live for the good things that were going to happen?

Then I thought about my life and why I was still here. The only thing that had kept me here for so long was the idea if I had killed myself, Mom would have my ass when she met me in the afterlife. Also, I had my children, and when I thought about them, life meant something again. My children had been tying me to this world and gave me a reason to live. When I had a chance to check out, during the time when I had pneumonia and almost died, I didn't. I chose to live through that. My children had repeatedly given me a reason to be attached to this world; they were my everything and the reason I simply had to live. But what about Manie? Did he have something to live for? Did he know he had reasons to fight for his life?

I laid my hands on Manie, thinking of what could tie him here. What could be his everything? I knew I had to be Manie's reason. I prayed to God yet again as I kept my hands on my child, and I explained to God, "I am his everything, I am his reason to be here. Without him I will not be able to go on and I can't leave because I have ties here. I will show him there is a reason to life and even a reason for pain. Let him stay here to teach me one more time why I need to be here."

I wanted to talk to Manie and whisper in his ear, but I knew he couldn't understand me; he didn't know the language of words yet. I continued to pray and I asked God, "Please speak to him and hold him. God, make him understand that life is going to be good because I love him. He has to make it through this, God, You know that."

Deep in my soul I knew Manie was meant for something special. If everything happens for a reason and the reason is based on the amount of everything you have to go through, then Manie is destined to be an extraordinary person someday. The essence of who he is and that he is meant for something more than just a normal life radiates off of him, stronger than the sun radiates light.

My deep thoughts and meditations were soon interrupted by the nurses coming to take Manie to the operating room. Russell and I followed him all the way down the hall and to his destination. Russell stopped before the doors; I continued to walk until they told me I couldn't go any further. I watched as they wheeled his crib past the doors. One of the nurses looked back at me and said, "We will take care of your baby."

I looked the nurse in the eyes and said, "Thank you."

I didn't want to leave the hallway outside the operating room but, like everything else, I seemed to have very little choice. Russell and I walked to the waiting area where all of Russell's family sat and waited. If I had been able to feel any significant emotion at that time besides worry, I would have been jealous of Russell because he had his family there with him. I didn't have anyone there with me. My jealousy would have been a wasted emotion though because, shortly after we arrived in the waiting room, my angel Mary arrived.

She walked through the door, I saw her, and I wanted to burst into tears because I knew then that of all the people in the world, she was the one person I could count on.

Mary and I hugged and, for just a moment, my heart released some of the tension it had been holding onto. The exhausting task of endlessly worrying was not one I would have to bear the burden of all alone anymore. All I had to do was look into my best friend's eyes, without saying a word, to know someone was physically there for me just in case I started to fall. I had never wished to share my pain with anyone but, without hesitation, Mary took a share of my pain to help me. Without her I would have never made it through that day.

Surgery day was the longest day in history. Technically I don't think it is classified as a day; it was more like a lifetime. It was not as if time stood still, it was different than that somehow. It was like being stuck in another dimension where time had started to fold on itself. I had prepared myself for being in the waiting room for a long time since I was told the surgery was going to last six hours. Of course after the first few minutes in that tiny little room, my mind was reduced to mush from never having had any real, solid consistency to form a realistic view of what was happening to Manie.

During the wait I often wondered if this situation were real at all. Nothing about that day felt real. I thought about how Manie was already eight days old. I thought about how it was St. Patrick's Day and I hoped that the luck of the Irish was real and I hoped luck would be with Manie. Like time, in the dimension I was now existing in, thoughts folded in on each other, one on top of the other. I wondered how the doctor was doing. I worried about the doctor standing there for so long working on something "as small as a walnut." Images of Manie laying there cut open and the doctor working on him would creep into my brain without my permission.

Six, seven, eight, nine, ten, eleven, then twelve hours passed and the evening passed right by me. At just a few minutes after 7 p.m., the doctor came in and told us he was done with the surgery. My heart sank to the pit of my stomach. I did not know if I should be happy it was over or be worried it took twelve hours! Right as I opened my mouth to ask why it took so long, the doctor spoke the words my heart had longed to hear: "Everything went well." I quickly shut my mouth and decided not to ask why it had taken longer than expected.

Then the doctor began to explain about all the tubes and incisions that we would see.

"Manie has drain tubes that sit alongside his heart and his lungs to help drain fluid that will build up," the doctor said. "Manie also has a pace maker and the wires from the pace maker lie on his heart and come out through his chest. Manie will be wheeled out soon and the nurses will stop by here to let you know they are taking him back."

"Thank you," I whispered as the doctor left.

A few moments later the nurses wheeled him by the waiting area where we sat. I got up as quickly as I could. Nothing the doctor could have said would have prepared me for the sight of my baby laying there with four big tubes and blue wires protruding through his chest, or the incision straight down the middle of his chest which was covered with white, cloth tape.

Manie did not look like my baby anymore.

Everything on him was swollen, from his eyelids to his little toes. The surgery was over, and he had survived. However, like the doctor explained, there was a reason for all the tubes and wires that were placed in his body. It would be awhile before we were sure he was going to make it. Just because Manie was done with the surgery did not mean he was done with being a baby fighting for his life. The hours and next day after surgery were the hardest. It felt like Manie was going to have tubes and wires protruding from his chest and belly forever.

It looked as if someone had made a baby blanket with tubes and wires and covered him with it. It was really hard watching the fluid and blood drain from the tubes knowing where it was coming from. During one of the doctor's rounds he explained there was a complication from the surgery. Manie had a leak in his heart which was a side effect from the atrial switch they performed. Despite having the leak, Manie did pretty well holding his own in the fight against time.

A couple of days after the surgery we walked up to Manie's bed side and, as usual, I had to check every inch of him to make sure everything was still there. This time something looked different, and it took me a minute to realize what it was. One of the tubes was gone! There, where the big round tube, as round as a quarter, had once been, there were stitches. I was upset that no one had contacted me to let me know they would be removing the tube, but my happiness overwhelmed any annoyance I felt. I knew that it was a good sign and finally there was some progress. Hope began to take hold then, and somehow I knew he was going to be alright.

The doctors started taking Manie off of the medications that were helping keep him alive before and also keeping him unconscious. It was scary to think that he was going to start waking up from this whole thing and not be able to understand the pain and what he had been through. For the first time in his life, since he had been born, he was going to have to live without sedation. As much as I wanted him awake, I wanted him out of it so he could not feel the pain of surgery.

Just barely a couple days after surgery, Manie opened his eyes. I watched him struggle to open his swollen eyes and my heart soared when I realized I was looking into the most beautiful blue eyes I had ever seen. I wanted to cry, but I didn't because I wanted to be as strong as Manie. I wanted to be strong for him and I had no right to cry; I was not the one who was having the physical pain.

I softly whispered to Manie, "Hi baby, I am your mommy. I love you."

I had said the words "I love you" to him hundreds of times since the moment he was born, but this was the first time he was looking at me when I said it. Manie closed his wonderful eyes and went back to sleep after that.

Over the next few days the rest of the tubes came out, and a feeding tube went in. The new tube ran down his nose and into his stomach. They started Manie on just a couple of drops of fluid through the feeding tube at first. He did not tolerate it well in the beginning. Problems with his stomach were to be expected since he was almost two weeks old and he had not had anything at all in his stomach up until that point.

His swelling was starting to go down, and it left his skin looking saggy and dry. He looked the size of a newborn baby again, and it was a relief. For the first time in a long time, I felt almost okay, but it was short lived. Just as I was starting to find some peace in this situation, Russell said, "I have to go back to work."

I knew we were having a hard enough time as it was paying the bills, but I hated the idea of Russell going back to work. We were only able to stay in Iowa City because of Russell's parents' help. Haley and Alex needed to be able to go back home; Spring Break was over and their school would not be understanding of their absence.

I felt torn in so many directions. Money was definitely a big issue for us and we only had one vehicle. I would have loved to stay with Manie every second of every day, but it just could not be that way. We went back home again and I felt horrible for leaving Manie there and being so far away. This time I knew at least I would be back there every day until he came home. I made that promise to Manie and to myself.

Our van was about on its last leg, but in my heart I know that ugly old van was running on my pure will power and determination to be with Manie.

CHAPTER 9

A MOTHER'S ARMS

"A mother's arms are made of tenderness and children sleep soundly in them." [Victor Hugo]

Manie was almost two weeks old and doing as well as any baby could when they had just had open heart surgery. Russell and I went back home to stay because we could not afford to be away anymore, and Russell's mom had, financially, done all she could. Haley and Alex started back to school and Russell had to go back to work. It was up to me to drive to Iowa City to see Manie every day and I was intent on doing so, no matter what.

In the past I had conquered my fear of driving. At this point I realized I had defeated my fear of driving around the town of Waterloo, Ia., where I was familiar with everything. Having to drive all the way to Iowa City gave me that familiar suffocating feeling I got when I used to be terrified to drive. I had motivation though; I had promised Manie I would be back every day to see him. I would never break a promise to him.

I woke up extra early the first morning after we had arrived home and got everyone ready to go and made sure they all got to work and school. Grif and I started out for Iowa City. I had travelled that road as a passenger more than a handful of times, but never had to drive all by myself. I gripped the steering wheel of that old rickety van as tight as I could, as if the harder I squeezed the safer we would be. Grif stayed quiet in his car seat as I prayed to God to keep the old van from breaking down, as it had a solid history of doing at the most inopportune times.

The first day we made it all the way to Iowa City by ourselves with no problems. Despite having a migraine, I felt awesome! I parked in the garage, took a deep breath, and got out of the van. As quick as I could I got Grif out of his car seat and we ran to be by Manie's side.

The hospital that had once felt like a big maze was now a monstrosity I was able to navigate easily, on my own. We reached the recovery room and we were so excited to see that Manie's little arms were moving around. He was up! Grif and I spent all day with him until it was time to pick up Haley and Alex from school. The rest of the night I couldn't stop myself from talking about how Manie was doing and how good he looked. I called everyone I knew and bragged, and I called the hospital every hour, on the hour, to confirm that he was still doing fine.

We did the same the next day, with the same results. But on the third day Grif and I went up to Iowa City, something was different. Life even felt different as we ran to the recovery room. For some reason, as we got closer and closer to the room, I slowed down. I put Grif down so he could walk on his own. I took a step and realized my bra was wet.

"What the heck is going on?" I said.

I could hear what sounded like a baby crying, but the cry was so rough and sounded so painful. I had heard cries coming from that room before, but nothing as sad as this. As I heard this cry, it felt like electricity was traveling throughout my body and my milk just started to flow uncontrollably. I realized what was happening in that moment and knew, without doubt, who was crying. My ears tingled from the noise and goose bumps traveled down my neck, into my back, and then across the rest of my body.

I picked Grif back up, turned the corner, and saw the entrance to the recovery room. Immediately my eyes latched on to Manie. He was lying there, free of the air tube he had once been using to help keep him alive. He was crying! I had not heard him cry since the day he was born and even though it wasn't his normal cry because of his sore throat, my body, my mind and my soul knew whose cry it was even before I laid eyes on him. I was stopped at the entrance of the recovery room from the excitement of realizing it was Manie making all that beautiful noise.

I grabbed my sweatshirt out of my bag and put it on, trying to cover up the leaking milk problem. I whispered in Grif's ear, "Do you hear that baby crying? It is our baby!"

He smiled at me and he gave me a hug. I felt like I was about to meet someone famous. I was so excited to see him and he was going to be awake without his breathing tube. I wanted the moment to be perfect, I wanted to remember the moment forever. I took a deep breath and started to walk towards Manie.

At first I could see slight movements from his crib, even from a distance, and then, when I got closer, I could see him lying there. I looked at the nurse and smiled and asked her, "When did they take the breathing tube out?"

"They just took the tube out," she said. "He will be watched closely to make sure he does not have any problems breathing on his own."

There he was, my little guy lying, there looking at me and breathing on his own. I knew Manie would not have any problems, he was strong and someone wonderful. Grif and I sat next to him, holding his little hand and talking to him. Manie laid there, his crystal blue eyes looking around. He looked at Grif and me with questions in his expressions. It was as if he was asking, "Where am I? What has happened to me?" His expression was so serious and not baby-like at all.

Looking into his eyes was like looking into a really old soul. The nurse gave him a pacifier to help sooth him. At first he really did not know what to do with this weird thing, but it did not take long for him to figure it out.

Manie started sucking on the pacifier, which was almost as big as his face, and he looked over at me and gave me a look as if to ask, "Am I doing this right, Mama?"

"You got it baby, you are doing it just right," I whispered to him. I did not want to leave that day and go home. What if Manie cried for me and I could not be there? I wanted to cry when we had to leave, but I didn't because I knew I would be back and Manie would be just fine.

On the drive home from the hospital, I thought about how I would never hear a baby cry in the same way again. Whereas I had perhaps though it an annoying, demanding sound in the past, I looked at it differently after that day. Crying is not a noise, it is a song. It's a song from a baby singing about something they want or need.

I promised myself then that as long as I could hear my baby cry, I would never think of his cry as annoying or bothersome. I would find comfort and peace in his cry and try everything that I could to make his song change from sad to happy. I promised Manie that as long as he kept the ability to sing, I would do everything I could to make his life something to sing about. My baby had a voice, finally. If he was uncomfortable or irritated, he could cry and let someone know he was not happy, and I would be there to listen and help.

As soon as we got home I started telling everyone about what happened that day. Manie was off the breathing tube and keeping himself alive! I tried not to think about how hard it must have been for Manie adjusting to breathing on his own. I wanted to keep everything positive for his sake. I would tell that story about Manie getting his breathing tube out to just about anyone who would listen. I was so proud of him and I wanted the world to know.

There are things that happen which hold special meaning, and we have to resist the urge to take even the smallest things for granted. Each of Manie's "firsts" were special to me – just to hold him or change his diaper meant so much. I know that those things are special the first time you do them with any child, but it was as if my feelings were multiplied ten trillion times with Manie, because I never expected to have the chance to do those things with him. You don't really know how special someone or something is until they are ripped from your arms, or your ideas about the way you wanted things are taken away.

Within a couple of days after the breathing tube was removed Manie was moved to a different unit in the hospital. They brought him to a unit for babies who would be going home soon. Seeing him in the new unit for the first time made me realize it was almost over, Manie had survived, and I had survived too. There he was, almost like a normal baby.

The nurse had even put a sleeper on him. He still had tubes and wires everywhere, but at least he was wearing clothes for the first time. He had his own private room now. It worried me a little to think that he would be laying in that room all by himself. The doctors must have thought he was doing so good that he did not need someone to keep a constant eye on him, like before. His new room was small, but he had a TV to watch and, believe it or not, he did watch it! It was so funny the way he would turn his little head toward the TV, listening and watching intently. I am sure he could not see it that well, but you could tell he liked the sound of the voices.

The second day Manie was in the new unit I came up to the hospital as normal and was standing there talking to Manie when a nurse came in. She told me in a casual nonchalant way, "You can hold him if you want to."

My mouth dropped as I couldn't believe how it seemed so meaningless to her. Just like that, with so little thought, she had said I could hold him – as if it were a tiny thing, even an unimportant thing, instead of an amazing breakthrough. I hadn't held Manie since that day before his surgery.

"Volunteers have been coming in and holding him, to keep him company when you're gone; he seems to really like being held quite a bit," she said.

I thought I would be a little upset knowing that someone else had come in to hold my baby before I had a chance to hold him. Instead I actually found it to be a relief. It was comforting to know Manie was being held and not just lying there by himself the whole time when I was unable able to be there. The nurse told me to go ahead and sit down in the chair. I was so excited and scared at the same time. I was afraid of where the doctor had cracked his chest open for the surgery. I thought if I moved him the wrong way it might hurt him. She put Manie in my arms and he and I just stared into each other's eyes. I stayed very still and tried not to even breathe.

Things were starting to come together finally. I felt so at peace holding him in my arms. The nurse came in and asked if I would like to try and give him some water from a bottle.

"We will start him off on the bottle, then eventually you will be able to breastfeed him," she said.

The nurse brought a tiny little bottle with some water in it and handed it to me. I could not believe what was happening – was I really sitting there, holding my baby, getting ready to give him a bottle like a normal mom?

Manie still had the feeding tube down his nose, and it would stay there until the doctors were absolutely sure that Manie was eating on his own. They expected it would stay in up until just before it was time for him to go home. I thought after never eating in his whole life he would be starving and would take to feeding like a fish takes to water.

I was so wrong. Watching him try to eat was like watching someone without legs try to walk. He struggled with the nipple and had a very hard time swallowing. I felt like a failure because he was not eating like a normal baby. Then I tasted the water they had put in his bottle. It was disgusting!

It was cherry flavored electrolyte water. The only way I could describe the taste of that water would be sour vomit. I asked the nurse if he could have something different in his bottle. She said, "No that is the only flavor of water that we have."

Can you imagine being a tiny baby and, having never tasted anything before, your first real meal was sour vomit?

Luckily one of the doctors came in to check on Manie and I told her, "He will not take this water because it is gross."

The doctor opened the bottle and smelled the water inside. "Oh my goodness! You're right, that is horrible," she said.

She firmly told the nurse, "Why do we not have any other water available? Go ahead and warm up some breast milk for him."

The doctor looked and me and could see I was overcome with joy. All of the hard work I had done pumping and saving my breast milk was going to pay off. The nurse gave me the bottle with the milk in it and I was so happy. It was still a struggle for him to eat and there was only about half an ounce in the bottle, but he drank the whole thing. I was so proud of him and myself.

Day by day, everything was getting better. I knew the hardest part of the nightmare was over.

After I feed Manie and he fell asleep, I laid him down and went to find the doctor. "When can he come home?" I asked impatiently.

By the sounds of her words she made me understand it would be awhile yet. I didn't argue and as I started to walk away, she said, "Maybe we can move him to a hospital in your town, that way he is closer to home."

I smiled and said, "That would be great!"

I was so happy at the possibility of getting to spend even more time with Manie. I started planning out the minutes of each day I would spend with him and I could even bring Haley and Alex to see him, and Russell would get to see him again. Everyone would be so excited!

CHAPTER 10

MY SCARED SECRET

"To escape fear, you have to go through it, not around."
[Richie Norton]

I never told anyone, but I was terrified of the idea of taking Manie home. Though I had longed for the day when I could, I was terrified of what would happen when I did; though I was an experienced mommy and had brought newborns home without fear, this time was different.

What was I going to do with him once I got him home? I didn't even know how to do CPR, and what if I went to sleep and something happened to him? What if there was something wrong and I didn't even know it? The thought of taking him home made me a nervous wreck. On the outside I pretended that I did not think about those things, but on the inside I was scared. I didn't let on about my fears because I was scared if the doctors thought I didn't know how to take care of him, they wouldn't let me take him home.

Every day I reminded the doctors about Manie being moved to a hospital close to our house so I could be with him more and so Russell and the girls could see him. The doctors kept telling me it could be a possibility to have him moved to a different hospital and every time I reminded them, they would tell me they would discuss it at their next daily meeting. This went on for a few days and I kept crossing my fingers in hopes they would finally agree to let him come closer to home.

Manie was almost three weeks old, and it hadn't even been two weeks since his open heart surgery, when I showed up as usual one morning at the hospital. As I had every day of his recovery, I arrived hoping and praying the doctors would tell me they were going to let him go to a hospital in our town. Instead one of the doctor's told me, "Manie can just go home in a couple of days."

At first I was totally excited! I couldn't believe it, this was about to be over! Then reality hit me and all of the "what ifs?" came flying at me, smacking me one by one until I was almost paralyzed with fear. I spent the rest of my time that day with Manie talking to him and secretly hoping he would understand if I screwed up.

When my time with Manie was over I went home and told Russell and everyone else Manie would be coming home in a couple of days. My panic over the idea of him coming home manifested itself into busy preparations for the big event.

I obsessively began to clean the house and started getting everything ready so it would be perfect for Manie. It wasn't going to be perfect though. Nothing could be clean enough or good enough for him. How was I going to do this? My secret of never being good enough and being scared to take care of Manie made it feel as though I was constantly holding my breath. Just when I would think I was going to be alright with it, another scenario would pop into my head and convince me I should be questioning myself and my abilities.

The only thing that would stop me from the never-ending task of getting ready for the big day was making sure I was in Iowa City to see Manie. I wasn't the only one preparing for Manie to go home, the hospital was tying up their loose ends as well. The day before Manie was to leave one of the student doctors came in and told me, "I have to take the pace maker out."

"Are you going to sedate him first?" I asked, concerned.

"It won't hurt him to take the wires out," the doctor answered. "The wires are laying on his heart, I just have to pull them out."

I watched as the doctor picked up the little blue box that sat on Manie's chest. Manie did not cry, as I had expected, but he arched his little back with each pull of the wires. As I watched, I cringed thinking about the wires sitting on his heart and what it must have felt like to have them pulled out.

The next doctor came in to inform me Manie also had to get his circumcision done. I did not want him to have one, but the doctor told me it would be better if he did. I did not think that kind of torture was necessary since he had already been through so much. I argued with the doctor over the idea of just leaving him intact. I only relented when the doctor said, "If he does not have a circumcision he could get an infection and that would be very bad for his heart." So I gave permission for the circumcision.

The next day Manie turned three weeks old and it was time to take him home. Russell took the day off work. We borrowed his mom's car to pick Manie up. We thought it would be better than having Manie riding in a van that could break down any second. I could not wait to get to the hospital. So many times before this day I would watch other mothers walk out of the hospital with their babies, and I was so envious. Today it would be me, and I would be the one with the smile on my face.

In my life I have discovered the more I try to make things go smoothly, the more they don't. On the way to the hospital we started having problems with Russell's mom's car. It smelled like gas so badly it was noxious. We made it to the hospital, but when we stopped gas spilled all over the ground. The car had a gas leak! We went into the hospital and Russell found a phone book and found the nearest car parts store.

Russell said, "I will be back when I get the car fixed."

He left me there in the lobby of the hospital. Immediately I wondered what I would do if he didn't come back, or if it took him hours to get it fixed. I was alone again, left to go get Manie by myself and responsible for talking to the doctors by myself. I sucked up all the negative, worrisome feelings and walked as fast as I could through the huge hospital, all the way to Manie's room.

I reached his room, car seat in hand, and there he was, almost completely free of all wires and tubes. The IVs were gone. The nurse was getting ready to remove the feeding tube. I walked up to Manie and softly whispered in his little baby ear, "You are coming home today!"

I stood back for a second just to look at him one last time in that hospital bed. It was a sight to see him unattached from the IVs and the wires. I had become a master at holding him while he was attached to the machines that when I picked him up out of his crib and held him, it still felt like he was still attached. It took me a few minutes, but I got used to the idea that he was free. I was able to walk anywhere I wanted to while holding him! It felt so normal and boundless. I never ever wanted to put him down.

I had prepared myself for the nurses and the doctors to come in bombarding me with a bunch of different instructions. Secretly, I was ready to pretend I knew what they were talking about and I knew I would have to listen very carefully, but sort it all out later. I hoped they had written everything down for me, so I could reread it later, when I wasn't so focused on keeping my face looking confident and sure of myself. I was sure they would have some sort of manual for taking home a child that has had open heart surgery. At least going over all the instructions would give Russell time to get the car fixed and get back to the hospital. Alas, I have never been so wrong in my whole life!

"I will get his release papers then you are free to leave," the nurse said. My jaw dropped in disbelief. Was that it? Where was the manual, where were my instructions? This couldn't happen this way. Surely she meant we were free to leave after, and only after, the doctors explained to me how to take care of a baby that just had open heart surgery, right?

My heart was pounding in my chest, drumming at a million beats per minute. Russell was not there yet and what would I do if I had everything all ready to go and still had to sit and wait for hours, maybe even days, for him to arrive? In a daze I began to put Manie in his little going home outfit, a white and blue outfit with a bunny on it. I took my time gathering all of his things, drawing out tiny tasks into minute-filling occupations. I watched the clock and the door and still, there was no Russell. I hoped the nurse would take her time with getting the release papers, but she didn't. It only took her a few minutes to come back.

I looked down at her hand and all I saw was one piece of paper.

"Here is his release paper and you have to sign down by the x," the nurse explained as she handed me the paper.

I looked it over there was nothing that even came close to giving me information about how to take care of Manie. The panicked feeling moved into a frantic state.

Then the nurse said, "Oh, I forgot something. I will be right back."

She took the paper I had signed and left the room. That was it, I thought, she forgot everything. I thought surely she was going to get the papers that would tell me how to take care of him. The absent-minded nurse returned a short moment later with a small, white card, a prescription, and a copy of what I had signed. The small card had writing on it, though not enough writing at first-glance to make me think it was an exhaustive, complete set of instructions.

"Whenever you give him bottles, mix a small amount of formula in with the breast milk. If you choose to just have him nurse don't worry about giving him any formula out of the bottle," the nurse explained, gesturing to the card which basically said the same thing.

Then the nurse told me she also had a prescription I needed to get filled. It was medication for high blood pressure. It was to help preserve the leaky valve that was created by the surgery.

"Watch for fever," she said. "Give him his medicine and here is the number to call in case you have any questions. You are free to go."

I don't know how long I stood there with my mouth open, but I was once again stunned by total disbelief. A hundred questions had already gone through my mind, but the only question I could verbalize was, "That's it?"

"Yes, that's it," the nurse said, with certainty on her face and in her voice.

I could tell she wanted to say, "You were expecting more?" As she started to leave I grasped at one of the questions floating through my mind, just to keep her there a little longer until I could gather all of them. "Wait!" I shouted. "What about cleaning the incision? Aren't there any special instructions for cleaning the incision?"

The nurse didn't even turn around to look at me as she said, "Well for the next couple of weeks give him a sponge bath."

I was horrified. Why was she acting like this wasn't a big deal? I realized I was on my own; once I took him home, it was all me. If I made a mistake what would happen?

Manie and I were free to go and no one seemed concerned that I didn't have any instructions on caring for this wee man. Well if no one else thought it was a big deal, then fine. They wanted me to go? Fine, I would. Manie and I would go somewhere else to wait for Russell.

I couldn't stand the idea of spending one more minute in that room waiting for someone to give a damn about us.

Again the nurse had forgotten something. Was she really that stupid and absent-minded or was she trying to piss me off? Before we left the nurse told me she forgot that we had to get his blood drawn down in the lab. Because of the blood transfusion during his surgery, they had to redo the entire newborn blood test. Russell showed up just as I was getting ready to take Manie down to the lab for his test. Every muscle in my body melted as I saw him walk through the door. It was about time something started going right that day.

Russell looked as irritated as I was, as if he had just gone through hell and back.

"I had a hard time getting it fixed, but I did," he said.

He kept trying to explain what was wrong with the car and how he fixed it, but my mind was elsewhere and I did not hear a word he said. The forgetfulness of the nurse and the idea I was going to have to take care of Manie and figure everything out for myself was the only thing on my mind.

I was also not happy about Manie having to get his blood drawn again. I carried Manie down to the lab. This was the first time I had taken him out of his room, and it felt weird. I actually got to carry him somewhere other than over to a chair to sit down with him. The moment I stepped out of that room, I stepped into a new world that I had never known before. In my new world, there were germs and cooties everywhere, at least according to my imagination.

As we were walking through the hospital, the realization hit me. I started noticing exactly how many people where there. I started to wonder if all the people I saw were ill. If they were in a hospital, it must be because they were sick, right? I wanted to shelter my baby so the germs floating in the air would never touch him. I thought to myself, how will I ever take Manie out knowing there are germs everywhere? What the hell am I in for and how am I going to protect him from everything?

When we finally made it to the lab, my germaphobic anxiety got worse. I wondered who the last person was that had been at the blood-drawing table, and what germs they might have left behind. I noticed a few spots of dried blood on the floor and the unsanitary, partially peeled, dirty stickers stuck to the cabinets. All of these images echoed in my mind.

"You can lay him down here on the table," the lab tech said.

"No!" I replied quickly. The questioning look in the lab tech's eyes prompted me to quickly follow my outburst with a plausible explanation. "I would like to hold him, if that's okay."

The person taking Manie's blood was nice enough and he smiled at me as he said, "Sure, you can hold him."

I should say, he was nice enough until he actually poked Manie and made him cry. Then, to me, this lab tech wasn't just evil, he was the ugliest person in the world! I know, I know it is just his job, but come on! My poor little guy had heart surgery and had been through so much already. The lab tech kept making hole after hole in the heel of Manie's foot because he could not get enough blood to come out.

I looked at Russell and said, "You would think they would have already done this testing before now, right before we were getting ready to go home."

I never wanted Manie to experience pain again.

Finally the lab vampire decided he had enough blood and we were headed back to gather Manie's things. As we walked out I told the nurse, "We are leaving now."

She did not even say good-bye or even look at me; she just said "Okay". Not "good luck," or "take care of yourselves," or, "you've got this!" or any such thing. Just, "okay."

She turned her back to me and walked away from us.

My son had been at this hospital for three weeks fighting for his life, and no one had even told us "good-bye" or "good luck". I was not expecting a farewell party or anything, just a little acknowledgement that we were leaving.

I remembered we had to get Manie's prescription before we left and, of course, the pharmacy was on the other side of the hospital. My arms ached from carrying Manie and all I could do was enjoy the pain. My arms weren't aching anymore because they were empty, they ached because they were full. It wasn't hard to keep my mind off the pain because, again, I kept thinking the whole time we walked about all the germs around us, and all the germs the sick people we passed must be exposing Manie to. I actually thought about having him put in a bubble.

The pharmacy prepared Manie's medication and gave me a recipe for his prescription.

The pharmacist explained, "You will have to have his medication specially made. Whatever pharmacy you go to will need this recipe."

It was one more thing to add to my ever-growing list of things I did not understand. I could not wait to get home and get away from the hospital. I do thank God every day that my son's life was saved but, like most people, I hated being at the hospital.

When we got home I wanted to stand outside and yell, "I am taking my baby into my house, isn't it great?" I walked through the door and felt whole for the first time in three weeks. It was a relief to know tomorrow I did not have to go to Iowa City to see Manie, he was already here!

I carefully sat his car seat down in the living room. Manie was asleep for the time being, but what was I supposed to do with him when he woke up? Just a few days before, I wasn't even allowed to hold Manie. Then, when I finally was allowed to hold him, he still had tubes and wires everywhere so I couldn't do anything with him. Now I was responsible for everything all day, every day for the rest of my life.

I figured at this point I would try to treat him like a normal baby. I would try not to worry about "what ifs," although, in the back of my mind, every time he cried I wondered if he was crying because he was hurt, or if he was crying because he was normal. Looking at him there sleeping, I knew this was going to be the toughest, yet most rewarding thing I have ever done in my life.

Giving him his medication took some getting used to. I never wanted to put him down and I don't think I ever did. I would undress Manie and there were the scars on his chest and stomach, a constant reminder of what he had gone through. At night I couldn't sleep for the longest time. I was in fear that he might stop breathing or something might happen to his heart. I kept his bassinet right next to me and laid in the same position all night, with my hand touching his side so I could feel his heart beating and feel him breathing. If by chance I did fall asleep, I knew if he stopped breathing I would feel it and wake up.

I know it sounds stupid to say I would wake up, but I happen to be the world's lightest sleeper. I was a light sleeper because as a child I was abused and always had to be on guard. Now I was grateful for that part of who I was, and didn't care how it was created.

After a few days I started being able to sleep for little bits of time, though I would wake myself up throughout the night just to look at him and make sure he was alright, and to feed him. He took to breastfeeding like he owned it.

When Manie was almost a month old, I took him to see Dr. Pranger. He checked Manie over and we chatted about the events of his birth. Then he answered some of my questions, which really helped me feel more confident about taking care of such a delicate baby.

In years to come there would be more pain and suffering, more surgeries and a lot of tears. However, together we discovered the wonders of the universe as well. You see, Manie being born the way he was opened my mind to the impossible. It was beyond my comprehension to know what it was like to watch as my child struggled for his life, but when I was forced to live through it, something unique happened. When one's mind is forced to expand in one direction, because of the universal laws, the mind must expand in all directions. Other possibilities reveal themselves and the wonders of the universe no longer are disguised by the limits of our minds.

The end of my series is less of an ending and more of a beginning. It is the extraordinary beginning of an important person that wasn't born to survive in this world, but he did and for a reason. Manie's story is just starting but already I can see that he is a teacher, a master manifester, a healer, and sometimes, he is just another kid. He is one of the most loving, caring people the world will ever know. He will always be a hero to me because, no matter what he goes through, he never gives up. Because of him I learned more about the universe, spirit, life and love then I could ever have imagined. Most importantly, he helped me see why all the trials happened in my life. He changed my point of view forever.

It isn't my objective to make you believe in a fallacy that everything happens for a reason. My intent has only been to give you tools to open your mind and let it expand in all directions, like mine has. By sharing our story you don't have to learn the hard way, like we did. We had our experience so you wouldn't have to. It's my mission to give you the idea that there is more to this world than what you see or how you feel.

There is something special in my Everything for a Reason series. In the same way fine art work or beautiful music leaves us to take away our own personal interpretation and message, I hope my series will do the same for you by prompting questions in your mind, which only you can answer.

The idea of conscious creation has been a cornerstone of this series, along with all the struggles I've gone through personally to bring me to a place where I have seen it manifested in my life. What I've learned through all my trials is that there isn't any secret to conscious creation, it is right there in front of you. You want to easily manifest money, love, and even the most trivial of material things. It's alright, it isn't wrong to have desires and acquire them. What is wrong is not letting things happen. To allow things to happen, you don't need to be positive every second of everyday, just find the one thing in this world so important it keeps you here no matter what. Find the one thing that is so special to you that, when you are focused on it, it washes away your fears and your limited beliefs, making it easy to accomplish anything. Discover your everything and then nothing can ever stop you, and you will begin manifesting all that you desire.

I also have discussed in this series a perspective which has given shape and context and relevance to everything I've ever gone through, and everything I ever will go through. I know I created a contract, long before I came into this world, which outlined the life I would live and the lessons I would learn. My understanding of my contract has been honed over time, but it remains the same in functionality – I know why I have gone through certain things, even the heart-wrenching things, because of my contract. When you understand your own contract, your life begins to make sense. This is mine, related to all I went through with Manie:

The Contract

A man stood humbly in front of a woman in a beautiful and peaceful place. The grass was green and there were flowers everywhere. As the yellow of the sun warmed everything it touched, they walked down a path set before them. They discussed the things they wanted out of life and why they wanted them. The man told the woman he had chosen to be a hero and described a horrific life full of suffering and pain. He knows this will mean his life will be difficult, but he also knows there will be rewards.

The man grabbed and hugged the woman's left arm tightly and said, "I know this life is going to be hard to live, but I choose you to be my mom."

"I can't," the woman said. "I don't think I am strong enough to watch you suffer so horribly."

"I need to do this," the man persisted. "There are lessons I want to learn and things I have to teach the world."

The man was begging, but the woman still wasn't convinced.

"How can I go into this world knowing what will happen to you and how much pain you will be in, knowing I am not allowed to stop it from happening?" she asked.

"You will not have to know, it will be a surprise and all the trials you will go through in your life will help save me and will make us strong so I can live. We will learn together."

"What if I refuse?" the woman questioned.

"You won't," the man said. And then, with a joking tone of voice, he said, "You can never say no to me."

He smiled and her eyes lit up with happiness.

"Mom, you are the only one who could ever love me enough to keep me in a world I can't survive in. You are the only one who can show me a love so strong I can't resist. You are the only one I trust to make me into the man I need to be, you are my mom."

"I will do it, son. I will be your mother," she said as she brushed the hair away from his eyes.

As she gazed into his crystal blue eyes she said, "I have only one demand."

"What is it?"

"You must promise me you will always hug my arm the way you do to remind me of this day, the warmth of the sun in this place we call heaven and remind me that everything happens for a reason."

"Yes! I can do that," the man said as he grabbed his mother's arm again and hugged tightly.

The woman closed her eyes and felt his cheek pressed on her skin, making a memory that would last forever.